Lima Beans for Breakfast

Here is My Story

Barbara Drinkwine

outskirts
press

Outskirts Press, Inc.
http://www.outskirtspress.com

ISBN: 978-1-9772-4742-1

Outskirts Press and the "OP" logo are trademarks belonging to Outskirts Press, Inc.

PRINTED IN THE UNITED STATES OF AMERICA

Dedication...

You are the man the Lord meant for me. You are talented, funny, loving, faithful and kind. Your encouragement has meant so much...you have earned your crown, my husband!

Acknowledgements...

The inspiration for this book came from my life experiences. My family was my structure and safety net. There were the great men of the bible revered as patriarchs. Today men are the head of the household or just good old dad. My dad is a true patriarch; a leader others want to follow, living his life as an example that is acceptable for others to follow. My mother was a remarkable and uncommonly brave woman. My sister is a shepherd...keeping the family focused and safe. My brothers are reliable, practical and adventuresome.

The people that came into my life through the neighborhood, school or social interaction are people that made an immediate impression on my life. They were colorful, zany, intense, intelligent, and immensely talented.

With extraordinary good fortune, my life intersected with theirs. Without them, there would be no memoir worth sharing. If our paths crossed today, I would say,

"Thank you for being my friend."

Barbara Drinkwine, Author

Website Address   **www.outskirtspress.com/ limabeansforbreakfast**

Email Address   **qtile.bd@gmail.com**

Table of Contents

Prologue

My dad was in the Menasha High School graduating class of 1942. He was eighteen years old and working at the Banta Printing Company even before his high school graduation. Pearl Harbor was bombed in a surprise attack on December 7, 1941.

Enlistment before the attack on Pearl Harbor was only 51,000 men. The day after, 2,400 men and women enlisted on that day alone. Before WW II ended, 16,000,000...yes, million men and women had enlisted in the armed forces. A great outpouring of patriotism knew no racial or ethnic divide...they were all Americans and wanted to serve and protect the freedoms of America. A million enlistees were African American and 44,500 Native Americans.

Eleven-thousand Japanese Americans were now fighting against their former homeland. Amazing for the times, 250,000 women had enlisted. Most of the remaining 14,000,000 were Caucasian men.

In the summer of 1942, dad enlisted along with over a million patriotic men. There was a progression of training for those entering Cadet school. They learned all the skills they would need to survive this war.

After his flight training in Santa Anna, California, dad went to gunnery school in Nevada. He went to advanced bomb training school in Albuquerque and there received his wings. His soon to be bride was there to proudly see it all.

He graduated as a Second Lieutenant in his Military Class 446.

My mother and father had married young just before dad entered WW II. It was during a brief leave that dad came home to marry his high school sweetheart.

My mother did not even have time for a fancy wedding or wedding dress. She wore a beautiful powder blue suit with white open toed heels. There would be no honeymoon but for a short time together in Pueblo, Colorado.

Now Dad would be entering the War as a Second Lieutenant bombardier on a B-24. From Kansas, Dad shipped out for his first assignment to the European Theatre in August of 1944. It was a week before he landed in Europe. Dad's home would be the newly built AAF Base in Castelluccio, Italy.

It was not long before the 451st Bomb Group(H) from the 15th Army Air Corps would see action. My dad, Jerry, was nineteen years old when Squadron 727 saw its first action.

The life expectancy of a flight crew during WW II was nine missions. My dad flew thirty-five missions in about nine months! In October 1944, Dad was bombing his first target over Augsburg, Germany.

On Friday, October 13, 1944 Dad's plane, the B-24 Liberator, 4-engine heavy bomber was hit by shrapnel.

Dad had just turned 20 years old. On one of his first missions, shrapnel flew through the plane and severed the co-pilot's legs. Dad had to hold morphine in his mouth to thaw it out. He had to hold his breath while maneuvering from his post in the nose of the Liberator to try to save the co-pilot's life. Dad tied tourniquets onto the co-pilot's legs and injected him with the morphine.

As dad looked up, the pilot, possibly being in shock, did not see the plane above him as he was climbing. There was no time to warn, dad reached over and pushed in on the control wheel to descend the plane. Averting a mid-air collision, the crew lived to see another day. Dad received the Distinguished Flying Cross for his quick thinking and bravery.

Dad came home in April of 1945. President Franklin D. Roosevelt died on April 12, 1945 as dad was returning from the war. He was home. I am transfixed as I think how it must have been for him a few days before on a bombing mission and now back home to this small town life.

My mom was nineteen and pregnant with my brother Daniel by the time my dad left for the European Theatre. He returned to his small hometown a war hero. He never looked at it that way, though. He said the heroes were the ones who did not return. My older brother, Daniel was born while dad was at war. I was conceived when he returned home in May of 1945.

My name is Barbara. I was a baby-boomer born as WW II ended. I grew up in the small town of Menasha. The men and women were coming home from the war. In my town, the paper mills kept jobs open for the men and women. Some did not return, but my dad did. So did his best friend, Artie.

My family lived on an island connected to the mainland of Menasha by steel drawbridges and rope bridges. The town was a thriving working class town. There was a post office, police station, library, two banks and the Woolworth Dime store. Our town had two large parks and several smaller parks, six churches with five schools that were part of the churches. It also had six public schools. The population during those years was around 12,000.

During the baby boomer years, there were so many children born, that the schools were bursting at the doors! Every public school teacher had well over thirty children in their classrooms. The parochial schools had fifty or more students in every classroom. Over time, Menasha had five parochial and seven public schools built.

In the formative years, Menasha and Neenah had canals dug to connect Lake Winnebago with the Fox River. The result was the formation of Doty Island. Doty Island had a boulevard of huge shade trees that divided the two cities.

A lock system connected several lakes and rivers making navigation possible all the way to the St. Lawrence Seaway and from there to the Atlantic Ocean.

Menasha was a paper mill town. In the early days, it was a logging town with resources for the building of the houses in the area. This small town is the setting for my story.

Writing our memories can be cathartic nostalgia for us, but a profound insight for family to learn the truth about their ancestors. It is important that future generations read what life experiences influenced and shaped their lives. These experiences can be traumatic, but many times are not.

Many more times the events that affect our life story are simple memories of deep and profound experiences that shaped who we became in real ways. My memories may have meaning only to me, but I think not.

I have found a helping hand during times of my life that turned me away from disaster and righted my path. Sometimes that was the hand of a parent or a friend. As I entered adulthood, I learned where most, if not all, of my help came.

Many times during my life, I made grievous mistakes. I ran from wisdom, turned down dead end roads and dangerous alleyways in the name of adventure. Only bad choices were the result. Why it took me over fifty years to focus on what really mattered, I am not sure.

Once I did, I vowed to explore a narrower path.

My family and friends, who may read this someday, will know I have not come to this stage in my life easily. I have been strong willed, impulsive, wrong thinking, disobedient, defiant and finally broken. Here is my story.

My Story Begins

It was 1948. I must have fallen asleep on a couch. It seems the couch was green, but I am not certain of that anymore. I was not yet three and it is my earliest memory. The eyeglasses came skidding across the wooden floor and came to rest on a metal grate. I remember explaining this to my mother when I was a teenager. She said it would be impossible for me to remember such a thing at such a young age. I insisted I remembered. Several years later, she relented and admitted that Grandpa Bill had fallen and his glasses did indeed go skidding across the floor. I always wondered why she insisted I could not have known that. Those were different times, and I was very young.

Memories, like the puzzle of a colorful kaleidoscope, twisted and turned during the next twenty years living with my parents. The huge white house we moved into when I was three rested directly in the middle of Oak Street on Doty Island. There was not one inch of that island I did not explore as a child. Every house on Oak Street had a family. I knew the names of every person of every family. I was incessant with my questions to the neighbors I visited daily.

"Where is your son, now?"

"What is his wife's name?"

"Are your grandchildren coming to visit soon?"

"What is a university?"

"Can I learn to play the cello, too?"

I went on and on until with impatient exasperation, they would say my mother was looking for me.

Growing up in the 1950's

After that first vivid memory of the glasses skidding across the floor, my most cherished memories were those of growing up on Oak Street. I was three when we moved to Doty Island. It was just across an old bridge from the Menasha mainland. I guess you could call us a middle class family. We lived in the middle of Oak Street that was in the middle of the mile-long Nicolet Boulevard. The boulevard separates the twin city of Menasha from its sister city, Neenah.

It was 1949, and I remember the move into the big house on Oak Street. My dad was sweating as he emptied the car full of heavy boxes. Mom and dad were a team carrying boxes inside and unpacking them one by one.

I was soon to have a baby sister, and I felt in control of my destiny. However much a three year old can feel in control, I did. Awestruck, I mirrored my parent's enthusiasm for moving into their first house. I remember the house cost $13,000. That was a huge sum in 1949.

Dad was home from the war almost four years now. He worked for the Banta Printing Company as a photo lithographer. I thought it sounded very important.

The Big House

My brother Daniel, who was 16 months older than me, had his own bedroom across from mine on the second floor of the house. There were three more bedrooms and a bathroom on the second floor. The bathroom had a white claw-foot tub, toilet and sink.

On the first floor was a sun porch, kitchen, dining room, living room and my mom and dad's bedroom. There was only a closet and a powder room in their bedroom. The powder room had a toilet and a sink. The kitchen had an icebox before my parents could afford a refrigerator. It had a worn linoleum floor and a full wall of cupboards.

Leaving the kitchen, you could go on to an unheated sun porch or into an entryway that led to the basement. We had a coal bin and a coal-burning furnace. That basement had clotheslines, a plug in wringer washing machine and my dad's photo developing dark room. It had a canning room for storing the garden vegetables. This room later became a chemistry lab. My brother got a chemistry set for his birthday one year and he set up the canning room as his private chemistry lab.

One year we got roller skates. They were metal with leather straps and metal tabs to hold them to your shoes. The skates came with a key to adjust the skate's length as you grew. Our basement was what we would call today, a multi-purpose basement. During winter or rainy weather, we roller-skated in our huge cement-floored basement.

The dining room was large with a mahogany dining table that took up much of the room. My mom always had thick pads and a lace tablecloth protecting the tabletop. Their bedroom was adjacent to the dining room with the powder room and closet.

Our dining room was special. The huge mahogany table had claw-footed legs and heavy wooden cloth-padded chairs to match. We played card games, Monopoly, and checkers on that table. Four children used that table to do homework. I can remember writing 100 times, "I must not talk in school" at that table.

The living room was as wide as the whole house. We spent most of our time in the living room or outside playing. Separating the living room and dining room were beautiful wooden colonnades with paned glass doors. My mother stored all her books in those beautiful colonnades.

Her daddy, my Grandpa Bill, avidly collected series of books by Somerset Maugham, John Steinbeck, Jules Verne and Agatha Christie. My mother was an avid reader. She said she learned that from her daddy.

The colonnades also held antiques passed on to my mom from her mom. We would give mom gifts for Mother's Day and her birthday. Those gifts ended up in the colonnades also. I would save my allowance to buy mom a present for each Christmas, Mother's Day, and her birthday. At one time, she had a complete collection of month angels. They had real gold on their wings. I still have a few of those angels!

The living room also had a lawyer's case with more books and an antique mantle clock. Growing up, we always thought that clock was haunted. Whenever the electricity went out, the clock would bong and bong. My sister and I used to hug each other closely thinking that clock was haunted. There had to be a reason for the bonging, but we never figured it out.

There was a console phonograph under the mahogany steps. It could play the glass records of the day. Mom and dad loved Big Band and the war music of the day. We would play Boogie-Woogie Bugle Boy and Five Foot Two, Eyes of Blue over so many times that there were grooves in the record. We knew right where to place the needle for our favorite songs.

Leading to the upstairs was a mahogany staircase. You could sit on the steps and look down through the rungs. It is on those steps; peering through the rungs, that I crept quietly to watch as my mom and dad placed our Christmas presents under the tree.

The big house had four bedrooms upstairs. In the hallway was a clothes chute. We would cram a week's worth of socks, underwear, jeans and shirts down that chute each week.

The bedrooms all had closets with very unsteady wood slatted flooring. We were not to go into them for fear we would fall through right to the basement. We lost many a coin collection and my rock collections down the walls of those closets. Indeed, they went straight to the basement.

They landed in the crawl space under the sun porch off the kitchen. No one ever wanted to crawl into the crawl space! It was very dark and this big house had spiders. It had very big spiders. My mom called them house spiders. Of my brothers and sister, I was the most terrified of those spiders. So, the coin and rock collections were never retrieved from the crawl space and they are most likely still there today.

Our Family Grows

My baby sister, Cheryl Ann came home with mom in July of 1949. I can remember her bassinette in the dining room. The bassinette was only a few steps from mom and dad's bedroom door and rested squarely against the back of the mahogany colonnade. Those beautiful colonnades prominently separated the dining room from the living room and provided privacy and space for our new little sister.

Less than a year after Cheryl was born, our baby brother, William Edward, better known as Billy, came home with mom and dad from the hospital. Now, Cheryl came upstairs to sleep with me. I was four and she just a year old. Billy was now in the bassinette behind the colonnade. Now there were six of us in the big house. My mother was twenty-five and my dad was twenty-six. Their four children were all under the age of six. Jerry and Joan settled into life with their four children. That big house on Oak Street was now home for four rambunctious children. That white house on Oak Street no longer seemed so big.

The Apple Tree

I began to explore our neighborhood...mostly my backyard at first. We had a stone walkway straight through our backyard leading to a trellis. There were seats in the trellis. We would play there for long summer days. We would play games like tag and hide-and-seek.

Mom had a garden and compost pile. There was a rusty incinerator used to burn all of the trash each week. A line of trees separated us from the neighbors in the backyard. There were many trees in our yard then. There was a pear tree, rose bushes, several box elder trees and even a pine tree.

However, no tree was as important as the apple tree. It was old back then, some seventy years ago. It did not look like any apple tree looks today. It was huge. Apple trees are not that big today. This apple tree had a trunk with a circumference of three feet. It was over twenty feet high. Many of my childhood memories include adventures in that tree.

We climbed it every day we could during our growing up years. There were branches so large you could nestle right into them. One branch was the queen's throne and one was the king's throne. There were three pretend bedrooms and even a castle chamber up in that tree.

I am not sure how old my brother and I were when we first tried to get from the apple tree onto the roof of our garage. My recollection was we succeeded sometime between seven and ten years old. Once we could get onto the garage roof, we set up all kinds of pretend places on the back flat part of the roof. We had to crab crawl over the steep part of the roof to get to the lower flat part. Then one of us would stand on the ground and throw up blankets, books, food and drinks. We pretended we were army men or cowboys and Indians, too.

Fearing for our safety, our dad warned us not to climb on the garage roof. Being short, I needed a stool to climb up into the tree to get onto the garage roof. My dad came home every day at precisely 4:00. My brother knew this as well. One day when I was in the tree, Daniel took the "getting down" stool away. Yes, at exactly 4:00, my dad pulled into the driveway. The first thing Dad saw was his little girl, Barbie, frantically trying to get down out of the tree. He caught me red-handed! Dad once again scolded us about the possibility of breaking our necks. However, we never stopped climbing that tree. I think my dad gave up trying to keep us out of that apple tree.

Frazzled

We were growing up fast. Daniel, Barbara, Cheryl and Billy were a lot of work for a young twenty-six year old mom. Whenever my mom had a doctor appointment, or had to go grocery shopping, she had four of us in tow. We had a dark green Pontiac. We all fit in the back seat with me as close to the door as possible. That was just in case I had a bout of motion sickness. As mom drove over the bridge from the Island, the usual ruckus would start. My quiet and sweet mother must have had quite the time with the four of us! As usual, we started shoving and pushing in the back seat.

My brother Daniel decided I should leave the car. He reached across me so he could open the car door. We were moving slowly as we approached the stop light at the end of the bridge. My brother started pushing me out the door. Well, our green Pontiac had these ropes on the back of the seats. So I grabbed onto one. He pried my fingers off and out I tumbled onto the steel grated bridge. I bumped and rolled across the lane and sat stunned on the high curb.

The only thing my poor mom could do was drive to the end of the bridge, stop for a light, turn onto Broad Street and come back up the side where I was sitting. She was crying. I was crying. My brother Daniel was not crying. Having by now missed her doctor appointment, my mother took us home. She fed me and put me to bed.

My mom just did not have the same temperament or tolerance as my dad. We would never get away with this if my dad had been driving the car. His hand-reach to the backseat was quite awesome to behold. I can only imagine how frazzled my poor mom must have been. No wonder she had periodic episodes of drinking!

2

Meet My Family

Memories of My Beloved Mother

My first awareness that our growing up years were not always normal was when I had come skipping home from school one day to see our massive dining room table filled with bottles. I was in first or second grade at St. Patrick's Catholic School about eight blocks from home. I was not sure what these bottles were but could feel the tension in the air. This, I believe, was my dad's attempt to shame my mom into turning away from her alcohol addiction. It did not work.

There were family secrets seldom spoken outside of the big house. Perhaps from stress or genetic factors, my mom began drinking after the birth of our baby brother. My Grandpa Bill was an alcoholic for many years. Now, my mom was, too. When we were younger, we did not know about drinking or what being drunk was. The doctor called it periodic or cyclical alcoholism. Once mom took that first drink, she could not stop until she was bedridden. We would pray for mom to get better. I was sure she would one day stop drinking.

Many times, our childhood was blessed childhood fun, island exploration, birthdays, and family trips. However, when mom was drinking, our life was chaotic. There might be one of mom's fantastic suppers awaiting us as we gathered around the kitchen table. Her supreme chocolate layer cake made from scratch was dessert for the week.

However, it could be cold cereal for supper as mom retreated into oblivion. As we got a bit older, we all took turns staying home from school to take care of mom. She would become very ill from a bout of drinking. I was probably in fourth grade and it was my turn to stay home and care for her. As I checked on her, she was very incoherent and not able to get up. I went to make a soup broth for her and propped her up in bed. I carefully helped her sip spoonsful of the warm soup.

She recovered and was once again on the recovery side of her addiction.

Then, the house was sparkling clean; our clothes were clean and ironed...which was no small chore in the 50's and early 60's. In the early days, my beloved mother had a huge load of work simply with the wash.

We had a plug-in washing machine with a wringer attachment to wring out the clothes as we took them out of the washing tub. About that wringer, my fingers went through the wringer a few times also.

After washing, we still had to hang the clothes on the line to dry. We used wooden clothespins on the clotheslines in the backyard or in the basement. For a family of six, this was a lot of work. When my mom was sober, it all ran like a well-orchestrated assembly line.

When she was not well, the clothes piled up for weeks on the basement floor. We put our dirty clothes down the clothes chute in the upstairs hallway and watched them go down the chute. We would then run down to the basement to look at the pile that fell onto the basement floor. It was our job to sort the clothes into piles of whites and darks.

White cloth diapers took up two twenty foot clothes lines in the back yard. There were four lines strung between two standing iron bars anchored deeply in the ground and connected with a top bar that had hooks to tie on the clotheslines. One line was men's dress pants and stiff-collared shirts. Mom's beautiful workday dresses made for a colorful display on washday. The last line had shirts, pants and underwear. Even at five and six, my brother and I had chores. Taking clothes off the line and getting all of the wooden clothespins in the clothespin bag was our big job; but it was always fun and entertaining for us.

I never knew my maternal grandma. She died from a blood clot right before I was born. My mom had no traditional help with advice, care of babies, or family problems. My mom missed her mother terribly.

Mom made it important for us to know about grandma. My maternal grandma's name was Anne. She taught my mom to cook and bake. My mom was at her best in the kitchen. She could cook the most delicious meals and bake the best rhubarb pies and chocolate cake, too!

My Grandma Anne had a sister. My mom called her Aunt Pearl. Aunt Pearl lived in Milwaukee where she was a cook and domestic for a wealthy family. They were the Dr. and Mrs. Madison's from Milwaukee. We took the train from Neenah to Milwaukee to see Aunt Pearl once. What an adventure that was. Aunt Pearl taught my mom how to cook like a French chef. Oh, my! Aunt Pearl was amazing!

My great Aunt Pearl always loved dachshunds. She brought both her dogs on the train from Milwaukee. We picked them up at the train station in Neenah. They came to stay with us for a week. What an adventure that turned out to be. Poochie was a female dog and Pretzel was a male dog. I took a liking to walking Pretzel every day. We laugh still today at Pretzel turning in circles before he did his job. Around and around he would go. Aunt Pearl would tell us to tell him to "get busy." It seemed to us he would never "get busy."

Even though we had a big house with five bedrooms, Aunt Pearl had to sleep in Daniel's bed. Daniel slept in the twin beds in my bedroom with Billy. Cheryl and I slept in the single beds in the other two bedrooms.

I gently knocked on Aunt Pearl's bedroom door. She said it was okay to come in. We were sitting on the bed laughing and talking. Aunt Pearl was always laughing....more a silly giggle. As we laughed, I threw myself back on the bed. Down came the bed...crashing to the floor.

"Oh my, oh my," was all Aunt Pearl could manage. I decided since she liked to laugh, I would just laugh. So there we sat on the broken down bed laughing. My Dad came up and fixed the bed for Aunt Pearl.

The following year, I took the train to Milwaukee. Aunt Pearl picked me up at the train depot. We took a taxi back to Dr. Madison's house. Never in my young life had I ever seen a mansion. Dr. and Mrs. Madison lived in a mansion. It had three stories. Aunt Pearl had the entire top floor. She had a kitchenette, bedroom, bathroom and a sitting area. The second floor was Dr. and Mrs. Madison's bedroom and the bedrooms of their already grown children. Because the Madison's were on holiday in Europe, Aunt Pearl let me sleep in their suite. The luxury was unbelievable. I slept so soundly all night.

Aunt Pearl and I walked the dogs to the park along the shores of Lake Michigan. I dreamed that night that I would be wealthy one day, too. Although that dream never came true, I felt like a queen the entire week I stayed with my Great-Aunt Pearl.

Grandpa Bill

Because my maternal Grandpa Bill had a reputation in town as a drinker, we were never able to have a close relationship with him. There was a time he was a boarder at the home of one of my mom's childhood friends, Ramona. Ramona's mom, who we called Mrs. Bunny, rented a room in the upstairs of her house to my grandpa.

My mom would take us there to see my Grandpa Bill. We would all clomp up the stairs to his room. That is the first time I remember being close to my Grandpa Bill. I remember him mostly because he had an unshaven stubble beard. He would take us on his lap and rub his rough whiskers across our cheeks.

Mrs. Bunny's house was very old even when I was a young girl. It smelled old and dank. It was always dark inside. My mom told me that was because Mrs. Bunny was very poor and never wasted money on electricity.

Mrs. Bunny had the most beautiful gardens with vegetables growing, fruit trees and flowers. She would depend on canning her fruits and vegetables to last her through the winter. She kept her canned goods in her basement. There were old creaky steps to the basement where all her canning was stored. Some of the jars looked like they were leaking. My mom warned me not to touch those jars!

Mrs. Bunny was elderly but was still doing needed repairs. My mom went to visit with her one day. There was Mrs. Bunny on the roof of her house fixing the shingles because water was leaking into her living room. At 90 years old, she fixed everything on her own!

Treatment

During the earlier years of mom's alcoholism, it seemed we were sheltered from her episodes of drinking. We had busy and frequent visits to our paternal grandma and grandpa. We were so close to my dad's parents. Grandma and grandpa were staunch and stable protectors during our growing up years. As we got older, they would take us on summer vacations up North. Looking back, I am sure it was to take some of the tension and anxiety away from two over-busy parents of four active children.

One time was particularly difficult for mom. She got very ill. Dad decided to talk to our family doctor. He suggested my dad should take mom to get some treatment for her alcoholism.

One day, when she was very ill, it was my turn to sit in the back seat of the car and care for her. My dad drove to a nearby city that had a specialist. She had to stay at that hospital for a week. As dad and I were driving back, I became very sick with motion sickness. I can remember my dad rubbing my back as I vomited out all the misery I was feeling into a roadside ditch somewhere between Clintonville and Menasha.

It was the first time I realized that dad had an enormous responsibility being the sole caregiver of four grade school children for the weeks that mom spent in treatment. There were many more treatments to come. Every time mom would come back home, she was more subdued and quiet.

It was not until many years later did I learn about the treatments. Those treatments could be part of an array of therapies. Common in use in the 1950's and 1960's was electroshock therapy. Doctors considered the treatments helpful.

My dad wisely spared our growing up years of any trauma it would cause us if we had known about it. I am sure he did not want mom to go through this. He talked to the doctor again, and the treatments stopped. However, it would be another nineteen years before her drinking would stop.

Considering my dad, whose dad was a city man and his mom a farm-woman who could make anything taste delicious; could not boil water if he tried. When my beloved mom was drinking, we had our first taste of eating out. At first, it was just the downtown diner dad would take us to after church on Sunday. It was the Prokash Diner. Later, we had an adventurous drive to Oshkosh to the new Jess and Nick's pizza parlor.

We were fortunate to have a dad who believed in commitment. He held the family together through the years of turmoil and craziness associated with addiction.

The Best of our Mother

There was no mother we four children could have had, who was kinder, stronger, or more intelligent than our mom was. Mom was what we would call today a liberal. She was beautiful and independent. She was not a disciplinarian. She loved our stories and adventures and seemingly never worried about our whereabouts. If we did something mom thought might get us in trouble; she asked dad to handle it.

Her best attribute was her sense of humor. She would laugh at the silly things we would do until tears of laughter fell from her eyes. She told us stories about her growing up years, too.

We would usually find mom doing a crossword puzzle or reading a book. After supper, we would go outside to play kick the can or stick ball. Mom would make sure that when the streetlights came on, we were in the house.

As my story continues, the reader will see that all who knew my mom loved her. She was a phenomenal mother with a problem. Many years later, she would conquer her addiction in the most surprising way.

I could write a book about her alone and it would be a hefty tome.

Memories of My Beloved Dad: My Rock

No daughter could ever have had a dad who was as strong, faithful, committed, and dependable as my Dad was. If Dad told you to do something, he expected you to do it. Mom was liberal; dad was conservative.

We would never consider talking back to dad. My sweet and kind mother was just the opposite of dad. We could manipulate her into doing almost whatever we wanted. I think she knew that and would often use the time-honored phrase; "Wait till your dad gets home; he will want to know this."

My dad had wisdom. He never compromised on his directions. If you were told to clean your room, your room best be cleaned or there were consequences. I tested this one time in my teen years. It did not go well.

Dad gave me fair warning. "Get your room cleaned, or you do not go to the dance tonight."

I put off cleaning my room until it was time to get ready to leave for the dance. Well, I thought, I will just do it tomorrow. So, I headed out the door to leave for the dance, I told my parents I would be home by 10:00. That was the very latest we could stay out in high school.

"Is your room all cleaned," my dad asked. "I will get it done first thing in the morning," was my reply. "What did I tell you this morning," he asked.

It was then I knew this was not going to turn out well. It did not. He went upstairs to my bedroom. He took off all the sheets and blankets from my bed. He took all my clothes that had piled up on a chair and put them with the sheets. Then he took everything off my dresser and put it on the floor.

"Now, when this is cleaned up, you may go to the dance," he said.

"But, dad I can do it in the morning…there is no time now to get it done," I said half sobbing.

"When it is done, you can go to the dance," he said looking directly at me.

I "threw a fit" as they liked to say. I cried and carried on. I yelled, "Mom would let me go!"

My mom just felt like crying with me, though to no avail. I cried myself to sleep. During the late evening before their bedtime, mom brought me some juice and a snack. She sat on the bed with me and patted my back.

I never did go to that dance. Many might think my dad was unfair. However, the lessons I learned from him were the direct result of any success I had in my adult life. Whenever I wanted to quit, I would think of my dad. My dad never quit…not on my mother nor any one of us kids…not ever. He was always there for us.

My dad was an intelligent and talented man. He could do anything he tried. There were things my dad did not like to try such as fixing the back screen door or a cracked window. He did not like to paint either.

Dad did mow our lawn. Therefore, it was our job to pick up the apples. Hundreds of apples had fallen from our big apple tree, literally, hundreds of apples! We had three or four large galvanized tubs we would put the apples into and then drag them to our curb in the front of the house for the garbage man to collect.

My brothers took over mowing the lawn as soon as they could handle it. When it came time for those things my dad would prefer not to do, he was doing the things he loved.

He loved to spend time with his best friend Artie. Artie was a pilot in WW II. He was an ace pilot able to do maneuvers most pilots of the day would not even try. There was a small airport between Menasha and Appleton. My dad and Artie would go flying for the day. One time, when trying out a few maneuvers, Artie flew under the telephone wires. He flawlessly landed without incident. My dad was much shaken up over that one.

They liked to bird hunt together. We had a nice pheasant or goose dinner when they were successful. Artie insisted on naming me when I was born.

They were shortly home from the war when Artie came to tell my mom she should name me Bobbie Jo. My dad overheard the conversation and put a quick stop to that suggestion. They all finally agreed on Barbara Joan. During most of those growing up years, my family called me Barbie!

Dad made friends easily. A family moved in next door to us when I was around eleven. That family became lifelong friends of my mom and dad. They traveled together, played cards, and even bought sites in an "own your own campsite" in the Dells.

Mostly, my dad loved doing his photography work. Many of his friends, during his middle years, were part of the Photography Club in our area. Dad would take pictures and then develop them in his little room in the basement. He let us come in to watch how he did it. He even made his own distilled water for the developing process. Then he would cut and matte the pictures. He won many first place awards for his photography.

In his later years, he combined his love of airplanes and photography. The home site of the National Experimental Aircraft Association better known as the EAA was in Oshkosh. He would travel to the EAA with his photography friends. Dad would spend hours taking pictures at the airshows that put Oshkosh on the world map. He displayed them on the walls of his apartment.

His second passion was taking pictures of old barns and houses. He has such a fantastic sense of color, shadows, subject matter and perspective in his photographs. Those who knew dad well will remember his photography work.

Memories of My Brother Daniel

My brother Daniel and I did everything together. What he learned, he taught me. What I imagined and dreamed, I shared with him. My brother Daniel was my hero. Other than the memories of that fateful car ride ending with me bumping across the steel grated bridge, he was a good big brother.

I always like to say that my brother was really my first love. Daniel was smart, practical, responsible and made friends easily. I loved everything he did. Life for me was just one big adventure. I wanted to do everything right now! I pestered him relentlessly, "Let's build a snow fort, let's go ice skating, let's go downtown to the ice cream shop."

Whatever he was doing, I wanted to do, too. I followed him around incessantly. It was all fine until he wanted to go off with his friends and leave me behind!

No way! I would tag along as they tried to ditch me several times. I can remember him and his friends putting me through their Boy's Club rules.

They made me do everything boys could do. They would insist I climb a tree, jump off a big rock, run faster than they could. If I did not successfully complete the test, I had to go home. They kept giving me harder and harder challenges they thought only boys could do.

"It's the rule," they would remind me.

I missed one challenge. The challenge was to jump off the train trestle bridge onto a pylon. The pylon was in the Fox River near the dam. We loved to catch crayfish there. I simply could not jump off that trestle bridge! I walked home feeling very dejected.

I complained to my mom. Unsurprisingly, mom said, "Wait until Dad gets home and tell him about it."

That is what I did. Mom and dad sat me down and told me, "You are not allowed to tag-a-long after your brother. Boys like to play with boys sometimes."

That was a sad day for me. My big brother was growing up. He needed growing up time and space to be with his friends. I only learned about his next adventure many years later!

My brother, Daniel, was an explorer always looking for an adventure. He and his friends explored the island as often as they had some free time. One summer, he and his friends ventured onto the train tracks that covered the island. They happened upon a trap door in the middle of the tracks. This was close to the Gem Brewery that at one time was a thriving business in Menasha.

Well, boys being boys, Daniel could never pass up an adventure. He pulled up on the trap door. Sure enough, there was a tunnel under the tracks. The three boys squeezed themselves into the tunnel. It led them to the inside of the Gem Brewery. The vats for making beer were still there. There were labels and beer paraphernalia that would be worth a great bit to a museum today.

Because they did not want to get in trouble for trespassing, they decided not to take anything. However, it was tempting for these preteen boys to own a collection of beer labels.

Rocket Boy

My brother Daniel was inspired to be an astronaut. He got a chemistry set for his birthday and his dream was to build a rocket. He studied about rockets and rocket fuel. His chemistry lab would be a good place to build his first rocket.

The day came when it was time to launch his rocket. He had three friends with him at the end of the boulevard. He chose this spot because Lake Winnebago was a good spot if things did not go as planned. He was careful when he planned everything needed to launch the rocket. He lit the fuse attached to the rocket. Then the four of them scrambled a safe distance from the rocket launch site. They did the count down.

The rocket did not launch. They did an extra count down, the rocket did not launch. Then, Daniel carefully made his way to the rocket. Just as he reached down to pick it up, it launched!

A picture of my beautiful mom and Daniel with his stitched up hand made the front page of our local newspaper.

Daniel is still an amateur astronomer almost sixty-four years later. He is self-taught and well educated in Astronomy. He keeps his friends and family entertained in the small town where he lives today. He loves attending Star Parties every summer. What a great hobby!

Memories of My Sister Cheryl

There are so many memories of my sister. During our growing up years, we were the best of friends. There were those times we were mad at each other for something or another. We had two very different personalities. I was loud, impulsive, adventuresome, and a bit wild. Cheryl was a quiet child, self-assured, content to stay at home and be with mom. She was intelligent and responsible. There was a three-year difference in our ages. This proved to be a barrier of sorts when we were growing up.

I was the big sister…her protector. When she was afraid of the neighbor boy, she would hide behind me while we walked down the street. She went visiting other neighbors along with me. She was my tag-along just as I was with my brother Daniel. Most of the time, Cheryl was a homebody and a very quiet little girl.

We were doing the dishes after supper and fighting over whose turn it was to wash or dry the dishes. This disagreement grew into throwing suds at one another…until Dad came out and made sure we got along.

When we were teenagers, we fought over clothes and sisterly advice. The difference in our ages affected how we acted. Times had changed from the 1950's to the early 1960's. She would laugh at the advice I gave. I was seventeen and she was fourteen but I was already a dinosaur in her thinking.

In the mid 60's, drugs started infiltrating even small towns like Menasha. Cheryl never had much to do with that, but did try smoking cigarettes. During her growing up high school years, there was constant peer pressure to smoke. She did not smoke very long. She made friends easily and has lifelong friendships with her high school group of friends to this day.

Cheryl met the love of her life in high school. She always wanted to be a nurse; and when Joe entered the Viet Nam War in 1968, they were first married. Cheryl was able to work when Joe went to war in Viet Nam. She loved nursing.

When Joe returned from Viet Nam, they had four children. All of them are successful, bright, and capable. Cheryl was determined her children would grow up to love travel and family. They had a motorhome they used for every vacation. The memories they made with that motorhome will last a lifetime!

Not particularly close during our growing up years because of the age difference, Cheryl and I became close during our adult years. She was in my wedding and we were having children of our own. She is one of the reasons I wanted to move back to my hometown of Menasha. She is the proof that the younger can teach the elder a thing or two. She and Joe just recently celebrated fifty years of marriage.

There is something wonderful about a little sister. They pull at the heartstrings of big sisters. Cheryl became a more grounded and self-assured adult than I was. She became the shepherd while I was the sheep.

Memories of My Brother Billy

Everyone loved Billy. He was the happiest little baby you ever saw. We loved playing with him and playing pranks when he was still in diapers. There was the time Daniel and I put raw eggs, whole shell and all, in Billy's diapers. Then we sat him firmly down on the ground. My mom did not think that was as funny as we did.

Billy had trouble learning to read in school. We never realized until he was in first grade at St. Patrick's Catholic School that he had amblyopia. Amblyopia was an eye condition that could cause blindness if left untreated. Discovery of new treatments were promising. We all learned that Billy was a smart, loving, carefree and caring boy.

His only problem in learning to read was the blindness in one eye. He had double vision in the other eye. Billy did his best to learn. He simply could not see. He wore a patch on one eye. The idea was to train the eye muscle to help the vision. Earlier treatment of his amblyopia may have improved his vision. Can you imagine his frustration with being blind in one eye and seeing double in his "good" eye?

Billy went on to learn very well. He said, "All I had to do is learn which object I was looking at was the real one and which was the double!"

With such poor vision, he could identify the make and year of cars from a block away. He learned how to do just about anything he wanted. He was gainfully employed, traveled with his friends, and met the love of his life in his early twenties.

I came to understand that Billy was probably the most responsible of us all. He was a rock. He was always calm and never judgmental. He had the sweetest personality any wife could ever want. He and his wife, Jan went on to have three successful and wonderful children.

The Fire

Another lasting memory as we were growing up was the fire. My baby brother, Billy who was now six found an old cigarette lighter one morning as mom was fixing breakfast. It was old and had not worked for a long time. Mom had it on top of the dresser so she could throw it away.

Billy climbed up on the dresser. He found the lighter and took it into mom and dad's closet to play with it. It sparked....the spark caught the clothes on fire. Our house was burning. My mom called the fire department and then called my dad at work.

The fire truck came very quickly, and so did my dad. Mom quickly took us across the street to our neighbors. We stood at their window and watched our house burn. The firefighters rapidly put the fire out.

Only mom and dad's bedroom, powder room, and closet burned. Mom lost all of her beautiful clothes and my dad lost all of his business suits. The carpenters came and rebuilt the bedroom, closet and powder room. Mom and dad got the Penny's, Sear's, and Montgomery Ward's catalogs and ordered new clothes.

None of us ever said anything to Billy. My frightened and a bit traumatized baby brother just needed a hug. It really was not his fault at all. Billy was a curious little boy who loved to learn how things worked. The cigarette lighter never worked for a very long time. Billy got it to work! Yes, in a most unfortunate way, but who was to know.

Memories of My Little Grandma Anna

Little Grandma Anna and Grandpa Ed were irreplaceable during our growing up years. We called her little grandma to help distinguish her from our other grandma who was Anne. Grandma had an old treadle sewing machine. She could fix any rip or tear. She would make us doll clothes, aprons, even dresses. She taught us how to use a wooden shaft with little nails on the top. Learning how to use this instrument was so much fun. We made potholders with the long strips of yarn we pulled out the bottom. Then we formed a circle with the long woven ropes of yarn and stitched them together to form the potholder.

One time in my teen years, Cheryl borrowed without asking, my favorite wool plaid straight skirt. She was talking to a boy on the phone that hung on our kitchen wall. She was very limber and jumped up on the cupboard to make herself comfortable while she talked. Mom told her to get down. When jumping down, my skirt snagged on the knob of the cupboard door. This put a three-corner rip right in the front of my skirt.

With angry tears and fighting over this for about a week, mom decided to see if grandma could fix it. My grandma could darn socks and fix just about anything. Grandma was a farm girl and the oldest daughter of twelve kids. She had plenty of practice and help learning from her mom.

As it turned out, grandma did fix my skirt. She not only fixed it, grandma fixed it so you could not even tell there had been a rip there. Now, Cheryl and I were on talking terms again.

Grandma taught us how to make homemade bread and apple coffee cake. She had a fifty-pound flour bin. One time mom asked grandma how she managed to use so much flour before it spoiled. Grandma told her it never spoils. When the flour got worms in it once, grandma just took the sifter and sifted them out.

Grandma was German. She made authentic German potato dumplings a couple times a year for the whole family. There would be ten of us around that table anxiously waiting for the dumplings. It did not matter that she made beef roast or turkey. All we wanted was the dumplings! The most important part of the dumplings was the gravy to pour over them.

These dumplings were amazing, huge and heavy with flour. Grandma taught us how to make the dumplings. Although I made them myself a few times, it was my sister and her family that inherited the task of making them for the family at least once a year!

Grandma taught us how to play poker. Here were the four of us kids around the table with mom and grandma playing poker. I remember when Billy was little he cried because he never won. Then, the next hand grandma slipped him a few aces from under the table. Billy won and he was so happy raking in the pennies from the middle of the table. He kept those pennies in a jar at home.

Mostly grandma was just always there for us. She took my part many times reassuring me life would get better. She even taught us to pray the rosary. We also learned this in school but it was more fun to have grandma show us how.

Grandma let us help her plant marigold seeds next to her garage every year. She had the most beautiful yard. She had a big garden also. We loved to sit outside on the homemade sling chairs and while away the day. That day was usually a Sunday. Hardly ever, in our growing up years, did we miss going the five miles to grandma's house. Every Sunday we would play cards as we sat around her huge dining table. After the card game, we all helped get the supper on the table. What wonderful times we had!

When my mom was in the hospital, my little Grandma Anna came to help us. When we were all older, we named her, Little Great-Grandma!

Memories of My Grandpa Ed

My Grandpa Ed was a very quiet man. It was his custom to sit in his chair and talk with his two sons. My dad being one of them. Grandpa would smoke a few cigarettes and then fall asleep. There was my dad and Uncle Eddy left to finish talking.

Grandma and grandpa took us on a two-week vacation when I turned sixteen. It was the first time I was ever away from home. Grandma let me sit in the front seat of the station wagon so I would not get motion sickness. She had read somewhere that if you could focus on something by looking straight out the car window at the scenery; it would alleviate car motion sickness. It worked! I did not get sick the whole trip!

We drove from campground to campground and pitched the tent. We set up the fire pit to cook our food. My younger sister and brother were with us. I was exploring the campground in L'Anse, Michigan, where I met some girls about my age.

I had to be sure to ask permission to leave our campsite. This one time, I really wanted to feel grown up and do what teenagers do. With my newfound friends, we were about to jump in the park ranger's jeep for a tour! I heard my grandpa's voice behind me as I was getting into the jeep.

"Barbara, do not get into that jeep!" Grandpa was actually yelling! I had never heard my grandpa talk much....much less yell!

"It's okay, grandpa", I called back.

"It is the park ranger and we are just going for a ride."

"You are NOT going for a ride," he said very sternly.

Back to the campsite I went. I remember being mortified that he would embarrass me in front of my newfound friends.

"Grandpa, they were just going for a ride," I said sulking.

"My dad would have let me go with them," I defiantly said.

Then, grandpa said something I will never forget. It closed the subject and I was not to say another word.

"I am not your dad; your dad is not here!"

"I am responsible for you," he said as he walked away.

You tend to look back at times such as that. I have thought about those times in my life when I had made some very bad decisions. One, just a year away could have cost me dearly. I could almost hear grandpa's voice saying,

"I am responsible for you."

Grandpa took me to college my junior year. It was the first time living away from home for me. He would drive very slowly on a two-way road. He took twice as long to get to Stevens Point than most folks. He would lick one thumb and then the other thumb as he firmly gripped the steering wheel. He did this at least one hundred times from Menasha to Stevens Point. I am not sure why he did that, but was just a habit I guess.

Grandpa and grandma had what we, as Catholics, called a "mixed marriage." Grandpa was Lutheran and grandma was Catholic. They never talked about that difference. They went to church every Sunday... grandpa to the Lutheran Church, and grandma to the Catholic Church. Oftentimes, grandma would walk to her church and grandpa would take the station wagon to his church.

My grandpa only lived to be seventy-five years old. He was in the hospital for a few weeks but hated the food. My grandma had to sneak food in to him. They finally rented a hospital bed so grandma could take care of him at home. In January 1970, grandpa passed into eternity. He passed with his bride of fifty years holding his hand and mourning his loss. There was not one day...not even one, that grandma did not cry and mourn for grandpa. She did this for almost twenty years. I miss him still.

We did not know exactly how adventuresome grandma and grandpa were until years later. They had a station wagon where the seats could fold down. They put a mattress in the back of their station wagon, packed supplies like a tent and camping gear, warm clothes and boots. Off they went to Alaska! This was in the late 1950's! We learned that many of the roads were gravel or dirt roads!

They took many trips. They drove the full length of highway 41 all the way from Appleton to Miami, Florida. They brought back seashells for us and a monkey climbing a palm tree.

They also drove all the way to California in their station wagon to visit grandma's niece. On that trip, they took pictures of the Rocky Mountains and the many parks they visited.

Many years later, I found the scrapbooks that grandma meticulously kept of their trips. It took my breath away to think they did all that travel in a station wagon. I miss her still.

3

Our Pets

Corky the Naughty Dog

Now that you have met my family, it is time to meet our beloved pets.

Our very first pet was a puppy. One of our neighbors down the street had a mama dog who had twelve puppies. She was all around the neighborhood asking if anyone would take a puppy.

"Well, of course we would," I replied.

When I brought Corky home my mom and dad said, "No, absolutely NOT"! I cried and cried. Mom and Dad relented and told me it would be my responsibility to care for Corky.

Corky was a black and white bouncy puppy. I loved him. He was my dog. Well, as Corky grew, his manners and his training did not grow. He was naughty, chewing up mom's new couch and wetting on the new rug...everywhere on the new rug. This did not improve. The straw that broke the camel's back came when Corky ran away yet again. He just would not stay in his yard. I chased after him but could never really catch him.

I came home from school one afternoon to find Corky gone.

"Where is Corky"? I asked repeatedly.

My mom said we would talk about it at the supper table. My mom just could not look at me as dad explained that Corky had to have a new home.

"Where is his new home," I asked choking back my tears.

"His new home is called the Pound," my dad explained.

That did not sound like a good home to me. I never saw my dog, Corky again. You could not hear one sound out of any of us at the dinner table that night. It was hard to swallow our food through our tears. Nevertheless, a few weeks later, Boots came to live with us.... for thirteen years!

Boots the Marvelous Cat

Mom and dad knew the four of us wanted a new pet. I am not sure where or how she came to join our family, but she was a marvelous cat.

Her name was Boots. She was a big female shorthaired cat. She was white on the chest and belly. She had a blaze of white on her nose, too. The rest of her was striped gray. She had a gray striped coat that extended half way down her legs and all of her tail except the tip was black.

Boots endured being dressed regularly in doll clothes. When she was irritated, her ears would be so pinned back against her head, we had to laugh. She did not like us laughing at her. She expressed herself with hilariously grumpy looks. Then, she would shake and roll to remove the doll clothes. More laughter ensued.

There were no screens on the windows in our upstairs bedrooms. That made it easy for Boots to go onto the roof of our house by way of an open window. We would run to get a blanket to hold stretched out near the ground just in case she might jump or fall. We would cry and carry on until our mother coaxed her back in the open window.

Boots ruled the night. She was a good mouser and often times brought us a present. One time it was a baby rabbit. The rabbit did not even have hair yet. We put the poor creature into a shoebox and tried to nurse it back to life. Boots never ate any of her catch, but she loved the hunting game. Mom fed her too well for her to eat the mice she proudly brought to us. I envied Boots her nighttime wanderings. I always wondered where she went. My mother would never go to bed without getting Boots into the house.

It was usually late when we could hear mom outside calling, "Bootsie... kitty, kitty, kitty...here kitty." Next, mom was in the kitchen cooking liver or shrimp to take to the back screen door as she tried to entice Boots back into the house for the night.

One time Boots did not come home. The whole topic of conversation at the breakfast table was where to look for Boots. On a blustery, rainy morning, I set out to look for her. By the third day, it was pouring cats and dogs. I thought that was an appropriate time to look for her. I refused to go home until I found her.

I crawled through the fence that separated our backyard from the neighbor's backyard. I called her name repeatedly.

"Bootsie, Bootsie, come here girl!"

I am still not sure what made me turn around to look that day, but I did. There was Boots trapped inside a neighbor's garage silently pawing on the window. I could see her mouth was open. She must have been crying.

My tears alarmed the neighbors as I pounded on their door. I must have sounded hysterical as I tried to explain through my tears. "Our cat is trapped inside your garage."

They came out in the rain and let me inside their garage. I made my way to the back where I had seen her. I now knew why she went into their garage. It looked like a mouse haven to me. I had to crawl into the attached coop at the back of the garage to reach her.

"There you are...good kitty." "I will take you home."

"Mama will make you some liver and shrimp." I talked softly to her, coaxing her to come to me. She did. It was when I picked her up I discovered her claws had been worn away and bleeding from trying to get out. Our poor cat was home again.

When Boots came home, life was good again. Mom cleaned her up putting salve on her poor broken away claws. Then she cooked her a big batch of shrimp and liver. Boots liked to stay in the house after that.

Catnapped!

Then there was the time Boots was catnapped. We were busy talking with the neighbors when my sister and I saw a strange woman walking down the street. We did not recognize her. Being that I was always so curious, my mom used to say,

"Barbie, you don't miss a trick!" Well, good thing I was curious this time!

As I watched the woman, it seemed strange to me that she had a heavy coat on when it was such a warm day. Suddenly, the woman bent down, scooped up Boots, and continued walking.

"Mom, mom," I yelled even knowing I was not supposed to interrupt adult's conversations. I was panicked enough not to care.

"Mom, that woman just took Boots!"

"What do you mean…she took her," mom asked.

"Really, for real," I yelled.

My mother took off fast chasing her down the street.

My sister and I made three of us running frantically down Oak Street.

"Ma'am, Mrs., lady, stop a minute," my mother hollered after her. The woman did not stop, but walked faster. My mother caught up to her at the corner of our street.

My mother simply said, "Ma'am, I think you have our cat. I think she is under your coat.

"Can I take her?" Thank heavens for everyone, the woman opened up her coat and handed Boots to my mother.

One other time when Boots did not come home worried all of us. We searched up and down the street. I went to all the places I knew Boots liked to visit. I could not find her anywhere. I do not know why I walked all the way down to the end of Oak Street. Boots never ventured that far.

This time I did. I found her in the backyard of the very last house on our block. She laid very still and stiff with blood coming from her nose. I ran all the way home screaming for my mother the whole time. Mom came with a towel to carry Boots home. Our beloved Boots was gone. We never knew what happened to her.

We buried Boots under the apple tree in the backyard all wrapped in a warm towel. I can remember that no one talked in our house for days. We all walked around wearing long faces and tears. Dad did not even make us clean our plates like usual that night. That is how I know he missed Boots, too.

My dad was an excellent photographer, taking many first place awards for his work. One award was for a picture he took of our beloved Boots.

Our Neighbors

The Meyers

Our next-door neighbors to the south were Mr. and Mrs. Meyer. Mr. Meyer loved to work in his back yard. When he knew there were two youngsters with a pregnant mom right next door, he put up a wire fence. I was so sad about that fence because I could not visit with Mr. Meyer while he worked.

He was building big round rock gardens for his flowers. As he plastered and rounded the cement and rock structures, he pressed seashells into the sides. He had a seashell fireplace, too.

I had so many questions. I would stand on my side of the fence and jabber away asking one after another. I seldom got an answer. Feeling frustrated, I put my hands on my soon to be five-year-old hips and said loudly,

"If you wouldn't be so crabby, more people would like you!" I barely got that out when my mother came to stand beside me apologizing to Mr. Meyer.

The next day, Mrs. Meyer made Mr. Meyer come over and knock on our door to apologize for being so crabby. I was peering out at him as he handed my mom a home sewn stuffed elephant to give to me from Mrs. Meyer. I have that elephant to this day...some seventy years later.

The Johnsons

Our next-door neighbors to the north were Mr. and Mrs. Johnson. Mrs. Johnson barely tolerated us, but really did love us. Mr. Johnson had the same drinking ailment as my mother. She realized that we needed someone to listen to us when times were not so happy. We would cut through her yard on the way to the school playground.

I would talk with Mrs. Johnson through the fence, too. I learned about her daughter who had gotten married a few years ago. She had a baby, so now Mr. and Mrs. Johnson were grandparents. I learned about Jerome, too. That was her son who joined the Marines. He served in Korea. When he came home, he had many medals on this uniform. Mrs. Johnson loved to talk about Jerome.

Mrs. Johnson had a beautiful yard and garden. She often helped my mom with advice on how to plant new vegetables. She had peonies and flowers in her yard, too.

Mary's Family

Across the street lived Mary's family. She was one of three grown kids. I especially remember Mary. She was sunning in the backyard with her high school friends when I came calling. "Do you want to see my new doll," I asked. I named her Annie after my grandma.

Mary asked if they could hold Annie. As I gently handed her to them, they started to fight over her and ripped one of her arms off. I knew it was an accident. I was too big to cry, but the tears gushed out of my eyes. I took Annie and ran home to show mom. My mom looked shocked.

"Can Annie be fixed," I tearfully asked. Mom did not think so. With hope, I pointed out that grandma could fix anything.

After church the next Sunday, I took Annie with me. We had a sad day at grandma's house that afternoon. She could not fix Annie's arm.

The Wilsons

Next to Du Frain's was one of my favorite neighbors. His name was Mr. Wilson. Mr. Wilson was a master gardener. His gladiolas won many prizes at the State Fair. Every year when the gladiolas had grown tall, Mr. Wilson would cut the most beautiful ones and give them to my mother in a vase.

I sure did not know it growing up, but all of our neighbors must have known of mom's alcoholism. Mr. Wilson's kindness to my mom was beyond being a good neighbor. He really cared about us.

He loved raising fish. He had more fish tanks in his living room than furniture. I felt sorry for Mrs. Wilson, but she loved the fish, too.

Joey's Family

These neighbors lived three doors down to the north of us on Oak Street. They had two kids close to our ages. Vicky was the oldest. Joey was younger and closer to Cheryl's age.

Joey was a messy little boy. He always had a runny nose and ragged clothes. Maybe his dad had the same ailment as Mr. Johnson and my mom.

My sister Cheryl and I were enjoying a Popsicle. Joey tagged after us hoping for one himself. A chunk broke off my Popsicle and plopped onto the sidewalk. Joey was instantly quick as he reached for it. I am not sure if I was just plain mean or not wanting him to get sick eating something dirty. Scolding him, I quickly stepped on it squashing it into the sidewalk.

In later years, Joey went on to serve his country. From all accounts, he was a good soldier. He went up in rank quickly.

Bucky's Family

Bucky was the "Fonzie" of Oak Street. His family lived across the street from Vicky and Joey. My brother called him a hood because he always wore a leather jacket. All the girls loved Bucky. He never had much to do with us because he was older than most of the neighborhood kids. His sister Susan was friends with Vicky. You will meet Bucky a bit later in my story.

Life-long Friends

A new family moved into Mr. Meyer's house when Mr. Meyer died. They moved onto Oak Street as I entered my pre-teen years. That is a story to reckon with and needs a lifetime to tell. These life-long friends will have their own chapter near the end of my story.

5

Unforgettable School Years

Kindergarten

There was a tough kid on our block…second house from the corner on the other side of Oak Street. I remember him for many reasons. The memories go back to the early days of Kindergarten. As I started my school years, my mom worried I would be too rambunctious at school. I was too curious, too adventuresome, and had a personality way much bigger than my diminutive size. I was what many called a loudmouth back then.

At five years old, I overheard my mom talking to Mr. Wilson across the street. She told him she never had to worry about where I was because she could hear me even if I was a block away. Mr. Wilson just kindly bobbed his head up and down. This is the year I met my friend Nate. The year was 1951.

I would be starting Kindergarten at a school just around the corner from my house. The Island was bursting with young children starting school that year. My Kindergarten teacher's name was Miss Nell. I loved her very much. One of the kids living on my street also started Kindergarten that year. His name was Nate and he was one tough kid.

He was a rough and tough little kid. We were playing Duck, Duck Goose at school that day. He tagged me. Jumping up, I ran after him. I almost caught him when he turned and ran right into me. I never thought it was possible to see stars. It was a "football hit" that sent me to the floor. I did see stars.

Miss Nell picked me up and held me on her lap. I cried and cried. Miss Nell told me I would be okay....and I was. That is my story and I am sticking to it.

As my mother told the story, Miss Nell had to call her about the lump on my forehead and redness around the mouth. Mom was convinced I must have been yelling and running around the classroom when I should have been walking. I told her all about playing a game when Nate's head hit my mouth. I told her I saw stars, too! I think my mom was doubtful.

During that school year, Miss Nell married. We had to get used to her new name, Mrs. Thompson. Mrs. Thompson was destined to become a Kindergarten teacher. She was wonderful with over-active loud little girls that still had to learn to walk instead of run in the classroom.

Not Quite Ready for Catholic School Years

The following year we all became "big" first graders with many of us transferring to the Catholic school. During those days, Catholic schools did not have a Kindergarten. Nate and almost half of my Kindergarten class followed me into first grade at St. Patrick's Catholic Grade School. On Oak Street alone there were about six of us attending St. Pat's School. Twelve blocks of young children on both the Menasha and Neenah sides of the boulevard swelled the classrooms of St. Pat's School. This was never a problem for the Notre Dame teaching nuns. There were almost fifty students in one classroom with one nun! Nuns did not have classroom help back then, but they seemed well in control. Notre Dame teaching nuns were well ahead of their time. They had the best teaching methods than most public school teachers at the time.

It was during that summer of 1952, I became very sick. Our doctor said I had the German measles. Our family doctor's name was Dr. Anderson. My dad was very worried about me as I had a high fever. In the middle of the night, Dr. Anderson made a house call. House calls were common during those days. He gave my dad some medicine for me to take. I recovered several days later.

By now, I was very anxious to get back to school. I loved going to school more than anything else I did during my younger life. The eight years I attended St. Pat's Grade School, there was only one day of the week we did not attend Mass. Then again, if Saturday was a Holy Day, we went to Mass seven days that week!

I excelled in first grade. I was an early reader and was given the job of helping to teach those who were struggling to read. It was the instructional method of the day to assign learning groups by the student's readiness level.

There were the Pennies, Nickels, Dimes, Quarters, Half-Dollars and Dollars. You can take a guess what level of learning the Pennies were and what level of learning the Dollars were. Notre Dame teaching nuns were some of the first to use grouping by ability to deliver instruction.

My first grade nun's name was Sister Mary Frances. All nuns had to have Mary in their name. For some reason most of us just shortened it to Sister Frances. She told my mom I was "gregarious." After having to sit in the corner with a dunce hat, I imagine Sister Frances felt I needed to have more rigor academically.

Sister asked me if I would like to teach the Pennies and Nickels how to read. She gave me a Catholic copy of *Dick and Jane* to read to them.

There I was, sitting at the long tables explaining what words were and how to make the letters make sounds. I would reprimand those Pennies something like this…

"NO, P makes P-P-P…not PA-PA-PA"! Poor Sister Mary Frances!

My beloved cousin, Carol, was in first grade with me along with fifty other students. I told Sister Frances that she must have made a mistake because certainly my cousin Carol, who was in the Nickels group, should be in the Quarters.

Bless her for caring! Sister Frances must have thought it was important to me. So, my cousin became a Quarter. I was a Half-Dollar and of course, I was not very happy about it. I went to Sister telling her that I was certainly to be a Dollar. She moved me to the Dollars where I remained to the end of the year. In that group was my childhood friend, Nate. The one who knocked me silly in Kindergarten.

Many unbelievable, hilarious and even sad experiences filled the school years from Kindergarten through my graduation from High School. Sharing them all would fill a book alone. Here are a few of them.

Second Grade and Beyond

My second grade year at St. Pat's was not as exciting and rewarding as my first grade year. I had Sister Mary Marie. She was new to the convent of Notre Dame teaching nuns. She did not let me make suggestions as I had done in first grade. In fact, she told me I must never talk. She made it a rule that only the top group of students who were well behaved could go to the school picnic in Smith Park.

Now, I must say that the school picnic is something every single Catholic school kid looked forward to every year. Apparently, I was not to go to the picnic. I cried all the way down the boulevard to my house on Oak Street. I sobbed as I cried out my sadness to my mom. Sister Mary Marie would not let me go to the picnic. Mom cried with me. Even parents did not challenge the Notre Dame teaching nuns!

Recess was always an anxiously awaited time. By fourth grade, most of us grew restless during the school day. It was a long day from leaving home at 7:30 in the morning and getting home at 3:45. We welcomed every recess. There was a short recess in the morning and a longer recess after lunch in the afternoon. The girls loved to play jump rope. Whoever brought the jump rope to school could pick who could play. Julie brought the jump rope that day and did not pick me to play. I decided to walk around and see what others were doing.

There was a big crowd of kids by the back fence of the playground. Wondering what they were doing, I went to see. There was a third grader with a daddy longlegs in her hand. She grabbed one long leg and pulled it out. She pulled out all eight legs one by one. Then she blew the body of the spider off her hand. My eyes must have been a big as saucers. Now, I do not like spiders, but I felt like crying for that poor legless spider! I had nightmares that night.

Three more memories from those years are my sixth, seventh and eighth grade years. In sixth grade, I had Sister Mary Grace as my teacher. She was very old. She talked to the chalkboard not to the students. I wanted to learn, but I learned nothing that year but rule number one. You must never talk.

As an almost preteen, I became very disobedient during that year. I broke the second rule of…you must never leave the playground during lunch recess. I did. I walked to the A & P grocery store across a busy road from school. There, I purchased a very long paper bag of popcorn with a dime from my milk money. I put it under my jacket as we walked into school.

When in the classroom, as Sister Grace was talking to the chalkboard, I began to flick popcorn all around the room to my classmates. Sister Grace turned around and saw me. She approached my desk, grabbed me by the ears and used her knuckles to scrub my ears up and down until they were sore. I think they called it, "getting your ears boxed."

I cried all the way home. I showed my mom my ears.

With a look of disbelief on her face she said, "I think you better tell dad about this."

As usual, at exactly 4:00, dad drove into the driveway. I could not wait to tell him and show him my ears. He did look at my ears. After all these years, I can still hear him say the words.

"Barbara, go into the closet and get the belt!"

"OH...but," I began. There was no talking to dad this time. Thank the good Lord that walking into the closet to get the belt was really the worst of it all. My dad very limply applied the belt as I lay across his lap. I will never forget his next words.

"Now, I hope I never, ever have to hear you were disciplined at school again."

You might ask, did either my mom or dad ask WHY Sister Grace boxed my ears? The simple answer is, No....they did not. Consequently, no teacher had to reprimand me again.

During my seventh grade year at St. Pat's, I had the most amazing nun. Her name was Sister Thelia. She never used "Mary" in her name. Sister Thelia was a rebel. During the first month of the year, she sat us all around a bulletin board that had each of our pictures on a folded and sealed construction paper envelope. She said on the last day of school she would give us our picture and the envelope. She said it would tell us what our future career would be.

I loved Sister Thelia. I was a rebel, too. I learned it was okay to speak up. It was okay to give your questions and answers. I sure needed that after five years of silence at school. I was very sure the sealed envelope would reveal the future profession I wanted most. Certainly, Sister Thelia must know my desire to become a movie star, or maybe a lawyer or doctor.

On the last day of school I anxiously, with great anticipation, opened my picture envelope. Now, as I opened the envelope, I felt my whole future was at stake. These words would reveal my future. I was to be a Kindergarten teacher.

"NOOOO...I do not want to be a teacher!" I was angry and refused to forgive Sister Thelia in my heart. Well, until in 1974 anyway. I became a Kindergarten teacher!

The constraining atmosphere of the strict nuns was both good and bad for me. Thankfully, the last year of Catholic School was eighth grade. That year it was noticeable we were all growing up.

Eighth Grade

We listened to Elvis Presley, American Band Stand and good old rock and roll. I bought a pair of Rock and Roll Saddle shoes with the allowance money I had saved. My saddle shoes were red plaid where the black is typically on a saddle shoe. They had a buckle on the back of the shoe! Oh, I thought I was so cool!

I had Sister Mary Catherine. She was a huge nun in height and weight. She taught us some foreign math called Algebra. It is the first time I had ever seen it and did not want to see it again. However, I did have to learn it and learn it I did. Sister Mary Catherine was very strict but an excellent teacher.

The boys in our eighth grade class were beginning to notice girls. One boy seemed to like me and kept turning around to look at a sweet girl. Sister Mary Catherine gave him a stern warning he was to keep his eyes on the chalkboard and not on the girls. She told him she had eyes in the back of her habit but he did not believe her. His name was John and John turned around one more time to look longingly at his girl.

In one very swift move for a big woman, she was at John's desk. She told him to stand up. He did. John was also a big kid about 5'10" and probably over 100 pounds. Sister Mary Catherine took him by the back of his shirt and the belt of his pants and literally threw him out the classroom door.

We could all hear him hit the wall across the hall. Believe me when I tell you, no one moved, no one said a word or gave a snicker. There was complete silence in this room of fifty some eighth graders. Yes, all in one self-contained room with one nun as teacher.

Sister Mary Catherine looked out the door and asked if John was ready to learn. As he came back in the room, not one eye was on him but on the books on our desks.

6

One Tough Kid

You may now think you know my friend from just down the street as if he were your friend, too. The one whose head collided with my head during those Kindergarten years.

Sandwiched into these sometimes painful growing up years was always my friend. Nate was my friend, perhaps in my mind only. I loved him, but he never really knew I loved him. Other than clobbering me in Kindergarten, my next memories of him were playing a game we called Stretch. As horrible as it sounds today, we played Stretch, with a real jackknife. The game went like this.

When it was your turn, you took the knife and threw the knife as far as you could but still within your leg reach. Where the knife landed, you had to stretch to reach it. You were out of the game if you could not reach the knife. Nate usually won those games. Thankfully, no one was wounded or missing a finger after this game!

There was a time he did not win. We were playing a game on our front lawn one late afternoon. It was the game called Statue. The game went like this.

The Spinner of the game would spin you around by your arms several times and then let you go flying. Whatever position you were in when the Spinner yelled, "Freeze," you had to "freeze" into that position.... like a statue!

Then the Spinner would come around to each one playing the game. The Spinner's job was to give you a name that represented the position you fell in and give a price to buy you. Then the bidding started.

"I'll give five cents for the pancake!"

"I'll give you one dollar for the rag doll!"

The Statue that was "bought" became the next spinner.

Nate started to argue with my brother, Daniel. The game of Statue got out of hand when they started to argue...and then fight. Boys could have a knock you down fistfight in those days. The worst of it would be a spanking when you got home.

I could tell Daniel was getting the worst of the fight with Nate...who was one tough kid. I yelled at them to stop. They did not! We all knew he was the toughest kid on the block, but my brother would not back down. I ran into the house, not to get help as the kids learn to do now, but to get a frying pan to hit my friend. I am not sure I actually hit him, but he went home. I got the spanking for that one!

Playing Marbles

I still wanted Nate to be my friend. We all collected marbles in those days. Most of the driveways on Oak Street were dirt and gravel driveways. They were perfect to dig a hole to shoot marbles.

Still mad at my brother, Nate would not come to our house. I went calling for him. His mom invited me into the kitchen.

I grilled his mom on my usual who, what, when, where and why! That is how I learned he was the second youngest in his family. There was Janet, the only sister, then the boys, Ian, Alan, Nate and Evan (who we called Tykie). I learned that Nate's dad worked at Banta Printing, just like my dad.

Getting back to playing marbles, I was confident I could beat Nate at marbles. He did not like that. We all had shooters, cat's eyes, steelies (ball bearings), and corkies made from cork. We had all the varieties in our marble collections. Nate did not like to lose his steelies. He was one tough kid, but he respected me when I beat him at marbles.

Nate used to give me a ride home on the handlebars of his bike. We would speed down the boulevard without a care in the world. It was during one of these rides that he told me something so profound for a ten year old; I never forgot it. As the conversation went, I asked Nate if he was worried about committing a mortal sin. That was part of every Catholic youth's teaching. Sin. You did not ever want to commit a mortal sin, because you could go to hell if you did.

Nate simply said, "I can be as bad as I want now, but when I am really old right before I die; I will tell God I am sorry. God will forgive me." That works for me, I thought. So went the life of a 1950's neighborhood.

The 1960's

A new decade burst onto the calendar. It was 1960 when we entered our high school years.

Nate and I were not in the same circles. He was a scholar and a football player. I was a good Catholic girl out of my comfort zone in high school.

Over the years, Nate came in and out of my thoughts. As I grew older, I did not change my impulsiveness much. It was amazing for me to see how much Nate had changed. He was a quiet kid, a formidable athlete. He was very bright. When I heard of his high school ranking, I was amazed at how smart this neighborhood scrapper was.

Nate went on to play for the University of Wisconsin football team. He also went on to get his doctorate in engineering from the University!

Then, I mostly lost contact with him after high school; even though he attended the same two-year college in Menasha that I did. It was an Extension of the University. We talked at a few class reunions many years later.

I saw Nate only a very few times in my adult years. One time was at my ten-year year high school reunion. I was nine months pregnant with my second child Brent, and ready to deliver any day. I should have known better than to go to my reunion.

The only thing that fit me was a grotesque purple polyester pantsuit famous during the 1970's. There I was in that purple pantsuit surrounded by big-haired, well-dressed classmates. I could not blame anyone for staring. I may have done the same.

My husband Perry was great. He was having a ball at my reunion. He just wanted to dance. He was out there dancing with anyone who did not mind his dazzling shimmy.

When I took a break from the dance floor, I sat down next to Nate at the bar. Nate was oblivious to those around us. He was just glad to see me. He was still single. I was divorced and remarried to my husband, Perry.

Nate looked at me as if I was a real human being when I did not even feel a part of the universe. There are many more tough kid stories and one here is ripe for telling.

Before our fifteen-year reunion, you were to write for a memory book. Each classmate who came to the reunion received the compiled memory book. That year we wrote about someone who you most admired during your high school years. Many of our classmates wrote about prominent figures from the 1960's like JFK, Margaret Mead and so on. I wrote about Nate. I did admire Nate the most.

He grew up on Oak Street just like me. He grew up on Doty Island just off the boulevard. He struggled through Catholic education just like me. Then, he BECAME AN ENGINEER...FOR EXON CORPORATION!

As far as I was concerned, Nate had life all figured out when he was only in fifth grade. He knew what he had to do to get into heaven. He was a hero in my book! He always will be. I bet he is still the toughest kid on his block!

Although I think he should appreciate a whole chapter all about him, I best get back to my memories.

7

One Memorable Summer

Our parents let us choose what High School we wanted to attend. Menasha had a public high school and two Catholic high schools we could attend. I knew my maternal grandfather graduated from Menasha High School as well as my mom and dad.

I wanted to continue the family history by choosing the same high school. As it went later in my life, my two sons also graduated from Menasha High School. That would be four generations to have attended the same high school. I was happy with my decision.

Learning About the Dangers of Life

The summer before my high school years was a turning point in my life. It seemed like I had gone from total innocence to being afraid of everything. Here are some memories of that time.

There was another neighbor down and across the street. I remember this as if it were yesterday; that summer before I started high school. I wanted more independence when I asked if I could go to a night movie with Vicky from down the street. My mom never said no when we asked to do something. I went over to Vicky's house to walk downtown to the Brin Theatre.

I did not know she would also be going with her boyfriend. When asking, Vicky said her mom and dad would not let her go alone with a boy. I was the tag-a-long on this night. I remember not wanting to look when I knew they were kissing! After the movie, they ditched me. I expect they wanted to do more kissing.

I wanted to take a short cut home. You could walk over a rope bridge across the Fox River channel. It was very dark, but I braved it alone. Once over the bridge, the dark, looming Wooden Ware mill cast ominous shadows in the moonlight.

I heard footsteps behind me. I wanted to run, but seemed frozen to the pavement. Someone grabbed my arm. It was Bucky, the "Fonzie" of Oak Street. All the teen girls on Oak Street loved Bucky.

"What do you think you are doing out here walking alone," he hissed. I had no answer but that I wanted to take the shortcut.

"Don't ever do that again," he said.

"I know some pretty bad guys that take this shortcut," he replied with a rough voice.

Bucky walked me right up to my door. My house was just across the street and down three houses from Bucky's house. He used to call me "short stuff."

One last time, actually the very last time I ever saw Bucky, he said, "Short stuff....never again....got it?"

Yes, I got it for about a month. A girlfriend from my eighth grade class called and asked if I wanted to go to the Neenah Theatre with her. Flaming Star with Elvis Presley was showing. I certainly did want to go!

"We will have to walk, though," she said. Off to the movie we went. All we talked about was Elvis on the walk back to my corner of Oak Street. She lived two blocks farther down the boulevard on the Neenah side. We stood at the corner talking for a while. Then she had to walk alone. I had to walk the half block to my house alone. It was a long walk to the middle of the block. The streetlights were on and casting a shadow onto the road.

For some reason, I thought of Bucky's warning not to walk alone at night. There was no choice. As I started alone, I noticed a dark figure walking on the other side of the street. My senses were on high alert.

I walked a few steps when the dark figure crossed the street. He crossed right in the middle of the street. I had only one thought.

"Why would he have to cross right there instead of going to the corner?"

Before I even knew what was happening, the dark figure passed right next to me. As he passed, he reached from behind and grabbed me. One hand was around my mouth and an arm was around my waist.

There was no time for me to react because as quickly as he had grabbed me; he let me go. As I turned to see who it was, the dark figure was racing across the lawn of the corner house. He was running with a limp. I was sure I knew who it was. He had been in Daniel's class last year. When I was in seventh grade, Daniel knew a boy who had a clubbed foot. The boy walked with a limp.

When the shock left me, I ran the rest of the way home. When I reached my house, I noticed I did not have the wallet I was carrying.

When I think back, I do so with wonder. I was more afraid of telling my parents I had lost my wallet than a dark figure that had just grabbed me!

I ran all the way back to get my wallet. I found it in the grass along the sidewalk. I picked it up and quickly ran back home. I cried myself to sleep that night knowing I would have to tell my mom. At the breakfast table the next morning, I told her something bad happened last night.

"What happened," she asked. I told her about the dark limping figure. I told her how he grabbed me. It will seem strange to anyone reading this today, but these were my mother's exact words.

"Who would want to grab you?" I had no answer.

She wondered if he had done anything bad. I had no answer other than maybe we should call the police. Mom thought that if nothing terrible happened to me, we would have nothing to tell the police.

"You should just forget about it," she explained, "Just someone playing a trick on you!"

My sister Cheryl and I talk about it even today. We laugh about it because what was I to say to her?

We decided it was mom's way of calming my fear. I was afraid for the rest of the summer. All I could think of was Bucky's warning...never again.

It was going on a month, but I refused to walk anywhere alone, even if it might be getting dark. My dad finally sat down and had a long talk with me. He talked about how to be safe when I walked alone. Eventually, I mostly overcame my fear of walking alone after dark.... but not really.

The Haunted House

I have a frequently recurring memory from the summer of 1960. This was the summer before my high school years. Some eighth grade friends and I were talking about the haunted house on the Island. The idea grew in our imaginations over the summer. Everyone on the Island knew about the haunted house. It was right across the street from the Banta Printing Company. An old man lived in that house. One time he came to the door of my friend, Sally, who lived on the corner. He had knives with him.

"Let me show you my knives," he said.

Sally was afraid and quickly closed the door on him. Later that year, the police came and took him away. Although the local newspaper did not mention the increasingly crazy activities of the old man, the police must have suggested treatment in a mental hospital.

Ever after, the rumors were that his house was haunted. We had the idea that it might be fun to break into his house and see if it was haunted. That is what we did.

Barry, Jim, Patty and I found the metal doors leading to the basement. They were unlocked. Pushing each other to go first, we pushed into the basement. There was a coffin. Not one of the four of us was brave enough to open the coffin.

We continued exploring the house. On the first floor was the kitchen. It was in the exact way it must have been when the old man had been living there. There were dirty dishes on the table with food crusted on them. There were knives and cowbells everywhere we went in that house. The furniture was from a time past. We decided we would go to the top floor and look out the cupola.

That is when we discovered the hidden stairway. We climbed the steps to the top. We opened a closet door in the first room we went into. Barry came up behind and shoved me into the closet! Then, he closed the door. What Barry did not know was there was a recessed floor! I grabbed at the door ledge and screamed,

"Let me out!"

"Please, let me out," I cried with a terrified whimper.

When Barry opened the door, there I was clinging to the ledge. He first laughed and then realized there was no floor. He pulled me up.

"I think I will be leaving, now," I managed still shaking.

We all left that house thinking, without one doubt, that house was haunted. We never went back.

Learning How to Make New Friends

My mom looked at a listing of summer classes at Menasha High School, and encouraged me to take a typing class.

"You never know, Barbie, when you might need typing to do papers and projects," my mom urged me.

"Okay, mom, it sounds like fun and maybe I will meet some friends," I said with excitement in my voice.

I did meet a friend in typing class that summer before my high school years started. She sat at the brand new electric typewriter next to me.

"Hi, my name is Barbara," I offered.

"Hi, my name is Lynn," she said with a giggle and smile. I liked her right away. After class, I told her I would give her a call. Maybe we could get to know each other. She was good with that.

I realized when I got home I had not heard her last name. I thought it started with a "W" and looked through the W's in the phone book with no success. The next day I apologized for not calling and explained I did not know her last name.

She laughed as she said, "Polish names are hard to spell!"

"Lynn is easy enough," she said with her cute giggle, "My last name is another story!"

"I'll just call you Lynn," I laughed with her.

Lynn and I were immediately friends. We took long summer walks through parks and around the high school. We laughed and talked about everything. What a wonderful friendship we developed that summer.

8

Those High School Years

Eventually, a small group of friends began to form. By the end of our first year of high school, five of us became good friends. In varying degrees, we remained close for many years. I like to call us the five Amigos! There was Amigo Mary, Amigo Elaine, Amigo Sally and Amigo Lynn. With me, Amigo Barb, we were the five Amigos.

However, those high school years were difficult for me. I was young to be entering high school. I imagine immaturity had a lot to do with the difficulty. I had just begun to mature in a female way that summer. I had gone from wearing a tee shirt under my blouses to needing a bra. My mom did not think I really needed a bra yet. Somehow, I did not think going off to high school with a tee shirt was what I wanted to do. Mom relented the week before school started and helped me find a bra that fit.

Most of us heard the iconic phrase…"Ahhh, you are a young lady now!" Young girls today will be relieved to know my mortifying experience of the past can never happen to you.

Girls used what everyone in my day called a sanitary belt. It was elastic with a metal tab in front and a metal tab in the back. We would have to slip the ends of a thick pad through these tabs. My periods were very difficult. I had cramps so terrible as to make me faint.

A month into my first year of high school, I fainted in Latin class. The school nurse had to take me home. My mom and grandma solved the problem together by figuring out what I needed to do to prevent embarrassment. I waddled through most of that year in high school. Sanitary belts would soon become a vague unpopular antique from the ancient past!

My First Date

Greg invited me to the homecoming dance. He was a very tall boy. I was about "five foot nothing" and Greg was almost six foot something! My mom and dad said being short was okay because of their song, Five Foot Two, Eyes of Blue. It was "their song" when they were first married. My mom was short, too.

This first homecoming date was awkward. I did not know what to wear, how to act, or even what to say. Greg must have felt the same. After the dance, we walked the entire mile to my house on the Island. It was cold in October. I wore pumps and a very warm, fur-lined coat.

During this long walk, I could think of nothing to talk about. I did not know Greg before this night. Apparently, his dad knew my dad from work. Greg's dad encouraged him to ask me to the homecoming dance.

We finally reached my house. There was a cement stoop leading up to the entryway of our house. I stood on the stoop and barely came up to Greg's chin. I think he wanted to kiss me, but he was acting a bit strange. He asked if I wanted to walk up to the corner so we could talk some more. We hardly said anything the whole mile to my house.

No, I did not want to walk to the corner. My feet hurt in my black pumps. I was cold and upset that I could not think of anything to talk about. I was polite.

"Sure, I'd love to walk to the corner," I managed.

We walked to the corner and back. Back up on the stoop I stood. Now what? Greg was just not ready to kiss a girl just yet. Then Greg said something to me that was so sweet. I remember it to this day some sixty years later.

"I had a good time," he said.

"Did you know that nice things some in small packages," he asked.

"Oh, I said surprised," feeling so much better. We said our goodnights without a kiss, but I felt better for having gone on my first date. Greg would be a great catch for some lucky girl in a few years.

Greg married one of our classmates several years later. Oh, and I finally got that kiss from Greg...a nice kiss on the cheek at our 50th class reunion!

Growing Up is Never Easy

So far, my feelings about high school collided with wanting to be grown up and wanting to go back to the safety of my younger years.

During my high school years, I made many close friends, dated many boys though none seriously. I lived for the time high school would end. I was not the boisterous loudmouth of my youth. I was becoming quiet and insecure.

Some painful and some thrilling, the memories of this time come flooding back. Many friends made the decision to choose Menasha High School rather than continuing on to St. Mary's High School. Either they gravitated away from me or I gravitated away from them. After eight years of being classmates, you would think I would have been more comfortable being with them.

Instead, I made friends with a new group of girls. We were the five Amigos. Lynn and Mary were probably the closest Amigos and became lifelong friends.

We stayed in touch sporadically over the years. We often reconnected at the class reunions many years later. For some reason unknown at the time, I felt comfortable with this new group of friends.

The Adventures of Growing Up

Lynn and I had an adventure our junior year of high school. We convinced our parents to let us go to a resort town about forty miles from Menasha. Lynn had just gotten her driver's license. She was adventuresome like me. Through "hook and by crook," Lynn convinced her parents she needed the car for an overnight stay in a campground in Waupaca.

We met some boys at the Indian Head Resort. Lynn went her way and I went my way. The boy I met was from a suburb of Chicago. His name was Lowell and I was in love. I corresponded with Lowell for about a year. The distance proved to be a big factor. Lynn met a boy from Appleton. That encounter did not even last past getting home.

I have a funny memory of that night at the Resort. It was the next morning when Lynn and I woke up in the car; yes, we slept in the car all night! It was a Sunday morning. What do two good Catholic girls do on Sunday morning? They go to Mass, of course. We changed our clothes in the bathroom of a gas station and went to church. The days of such innocence is difficult to find today.

Lynn went on to marry her college sweetheart…a Menasha boy! We talk yet to this day. Our classmates meet for breakfast once a month. Lynn and I could pick up right where we left off at any time!

I had a lot in common with my friend, Mary. Her mother was an alcoholic also. Mary and I took many long walks during the summer breaks of our high school years. Mary was an artist and so, I learned a lot about art. She painted a symbolic picture for me of a sunny yellow flower whose blossom reached skyward, but the leaves turned down. She said it meant part of my life would be sunny and part would be tragic. She could not have been more right. I still have that picture to-day some 60 years later. Mary paints mostly desert landscapes today. She is an excellent artist and friend.

Mary and I often walked with two boys from our class. She was going steady with Bill and I liked Jeff. It was typical of friendship during the middle of the 60's. We enjoyed talking and just hanging out. Those were such good memories from my high school years.

My First Kiss

My sophomore year, I was invited to homecoming by a very nice young man. His name was Vince. Vince was the first boy to kiss me. I managed not to meet the requirements of "sweet sixteen and never kissed". I had just turned fifteen a few months before.

Vince went on to marry one of the five Amigos, Elaine. He became a Lutheran minister. They had two children and adopted two more as they built their lives around ministry. Elaine loved every minute of be-ing a mom and helping at their church.

Amigo Sally

Amigo Sally was one of the five who walked to the beat of her own drum. She was a very self-assured girl. She had a Wallflowers party at her house for all the group of friends who were not asked to homecoming our junior year. We were the Wallflowers!

There must have been eight boys and eight girls there. What a wonderful time we had as we shared games like "pass the lifesaver on a toothpick" to the mouth of the boy next to you. Now, Sally truly was a liberal back then and still a liberal to this very day. I just loved her for her courage, intelligence, and talent.

Besides that wonder-filled Wallflower party, I remember Sally for walking me home half way when it was time to leave. I lived on the Island and she lived only a few blocks from the high school. I was very worried about walking alone since my encounter the summer before high school.

We were crossing the bridge when she said,

"This is more than half way, I better get back home!"

Discernment

Just as she said that, a carful of boys stopped and wondered if we wanted a ride. Being full of whatever mischievousness teenage girls are full of, we jumped into the back seat. I realized almost too late that these were not Menasha boys at all. From the back seat of the car, I looked up into the rearview mirror. I saw pure evil looking back at me. Terrified, I made some silly excuse while shoving Sally out the door.

"We have to go back for something we forgot," was all I could manage. I could hear the boys laughing as the car pulled away.

Shaking, I explained to her it was not a good idea for us to get in with boys we did not know. We stayed in the middle of the bridge for a long time talking until I had the courage to run for home. I never ran so fast in my whole life certain that car of boys was parked on our street waiting for me. This was one time I am sure Jesus was looking out for me.

High School Fun

The best memories from high school were the park dances. There were two park dances a week during the summer. Jerry-B spun the records for these dances. It was all the wonderful early 60's Rock and Roll like the Hand Jive, the Stroll, and the Twist! If we were lucky enough to have a handsome boy ask us to dance a slow dance, it would be a night well remembered!

With two high schools in this small town, you can imagine the teen-agers crammed into an upstairs dance floor. There was no fire code in those days. We called the building the Mem. This memorial building in Smith Park honored the men and women from WW II. All the winter dances were there.

The pavilion was an all open outdoor pavilion. It is where we danced during the summer months. Everyone knew everyone or at least met those that came from every school around. The park dances were famous during those days. American Bandstand inspired a love of Rock and Roll and teen friendship.

It was at a park dance I met Pete. He asked me to prom. Pete was from Appleton. The Menasha boys were not happy with Appleton boys coming to our prom. Pete was handsome and a very good dancer. I was out of his league. He was more sophisticated than I was. I have all the prom paraphernalia of the day. We had prom books that others could sign. The theme of our prom was Moonlight and Roses.

I kept the napkins and program with the theme boldly on them. Pete and I went to the post prom parties and then out to the lighthouse. That is where everyone went after the prom. It was the perfect place to make out! We did a bit of that, but I was too immature for anything more than kissing.

By my senior year of high school, I was beginning to like boys....more than just friends who were boys. I started dating, but nothing serious. Mary and Bill had broken up for over a year now. It was Bill who walked me home from a park dance one night. As we walked onto the porch, I could tell he wanted to kiss me. I was very unsure of kissing and was new to liking boys more than friends. Bill never did kiss me that night. Although, we did meet one more time before I left Menasha for my junior year of college.

Those were the crazy, hazy, lazy days of high school. Although there are so many more stories to tell, these days were coming to a rapid end. I was truly excited for a new chapter in my life to unfold. Our graduation day came and passed. I began working summers for the Banta Printing Company to help pay my way through college.

9

College Years and Heartbreak

My First Real Love

My college years began in 1964. I had just graduated from Menasha High School and feeling truly emancipated. The college was about five miles from my home on the Island. For the first few weeks, my dad dropped me off on his way to work. My whole being was looking for a new adventure. I long ago had grown to love learning, so falsely thought grades would be no problem. I was looking to have fun and meet new friends.

Maybe I would even find my first steady boyfriend. I did! His name was Jim and I fell head over heels in love with this boy caught between boyhood and manhood. He had blond hair like myself. He was serious about getting a college education. Like me, he may have been wishing to meet that steady girlfriend who also eluded him in high school.

For me, Jim was the first of many things. He was my first steady boyfriend, my best friend, and my transportation to school. I still had not bothered to get serious about learning how to drive, so Jim would pick me up. We did everything together. He was the first to kiss me with young lust. We were inseparable that first year of college.

The summer before transferring to my alma mater, Stevens Point State University, Jim was suddenly distant and distracted. Then he broke up with me. I was Catholic and he was Methodist. His parents told him he could never marry me. They ended up sending Jim far away to the West Coast.

Completely and inconsolably miserable, I cried every day and was angry with God for sending Jim away. My parents did not know what to do with me.

Getting involved at the Extension made the days less painful. I was a cheerleader, not a talented cheerleader, but it was an honor to cheer on the first basketball team at the Extension in 1965.

Joining every club and activity helped me not to cry myself to sleep as often. After adding VP of our class of 1965, VP of the Fine Arts Club, and active in the Drama Club, no wonder my grades were suffering. Looking back, I see this was a way to fill the loneliness and pain of Jim's swift departure from my life.

Rebound

I started dating a young man who could play the guitar and sing the Folk Music of the day. You might remember groups such as Peter, Paul and Mary, Bob Dylan, Pete Seeger, Joan Baez, Arlo Guthrie, John Denver, Johnny Rivers, and the Everly Brothers to name a few. Those were the days of Woodstock.

Writing poetry about this new boyfriend's family was one way to convince myself I could love again. My new steady kept asking me what I would like for Christmas. I told him boots....I needed boots.

"Boots," he asked. "Yes, boots," I stubbornly said.

I never would have asked Jim for boots....never! As much as my heart hurt, I had to tell my new steady it was time for me to move on. With me going away to Stevens Point State College next year, our relationship would never last. It was hard to see the disappointment on his face. I think the ache in my heart for Jim was just not going to heal. Yes, as I write this some fifty-six years later, there are tears threatening to spill out.

A Glimpse of What Could Have Been

The summer was almost over and my job at Banta Printing was finished. I would soon be living away from home for the first time in my life. The late summer day was warm and full of promise. I went out to sit under the apple tree of my growing up years. I hugged the rough barked trunk tightly.

The apprehensions of leaving home were totally lost in the excitement of a great experience. I never expected that evening I would experience an unforgettable moment that has and will continue to linger sweetly in the deep recesses of my memories.

That weekend, I coaxed my life-long friend, Sandra, whom you will meet later in my story, into driving out to the Raveno Dance Hall. It was the local hot spot. The dance halls of the sixties are to be revered. You could dance to the Beatles, Righteous Brothers, the Animals, and so many more. The music was great but not as great as being able to drink beer. I learned I could handle beer if I mixed it half-and-half! That would be half beer, half Coca Cola! "Try it, you might like it!"

Sandra had not really wanted to go that night. She had to sing in the church choir in the morning. I made a promise that I would leave with her when she wanted to go home. If she had not agreed to go with me, I would have lost one of the finest times of my life. The Raveno was the place to go and I wanted to have a good time before leaving for Point on Monday.

I wanted to meet up with some high school friends from two years ago to see where they were off to in the fall.

"Can't we stay for a least a couple hours," I begged Sandra. I knew the answer even before asking. I knew it was not fair to go with Sandra and then leave her at the table while I danced and flirted. She had not approved of my break up with my steady a few weeks ago. She knew him and thought we should not have broken up.

I almost agreed to go home with her after doing a fast dance together. In the sixties, girls would dance fast dances together while we waited for a good-looking boy to cut in.

Out of nowhere, my high school friend Bill walked up to me and said, "Hi, long time no see!"

Bill was that same Bill who had gone steady with Amigo Mary and had walked me home from the park dances. He was a friend I greatly admired. He was always winning awards for math and science. He would walk out to the Island during the summer months and we would go for long walks. We would just talk about what life might bring.

Bill was that same boy who had gently led me away from an embarrassing situation one summer of our high school years.

My mom had been drinking. She staggered to the door when Bill had walked me home, obviously slurring her words of greeting to Bill. With a gentle hand on my shoulder, I learned something about true friendship that night. He told me not to worry about the situation that he understood. You just do not forget friends like that....not ever.

Now, two years past our high school graduation, I see my friend again, "What are you up to this next year, Bill," I smiled up at him.

"Would you like to dance," he smiled back. We did. I must have forgotten the time and my friend Sandra. I managed to learn he would be transferring to UW-Minnesota in St. Paul. He was studying entomology.

"We have to go, you promised," Sandra hissed from behind us.

"I know, Sandra, I know; but this is really great seeing Bill."

"Please, just a little longer," I pleaded. Sandra became quite upset that I had not come back to talk with her for over an hour....and I could not blame her at all.

"Ten minutes...that's it and I am leaving...and YOU ARE COMING WITH ME," Sandra insisted.

Bill broke the tension with a casual, "Let's go outside and talk a bit then."

"I am having the best time I can remember in a very long time," I wanted Bill to know.

We talked about the times of our youthful escapades and laughed. I knew Sandra was very upset. She was already in the car and had come back to remind me it was time to go. I think she even started the car engine.

"I have to go, Bill," I said with urgency in my voice. With more than urgency, a true sadness in my voice, I asked,

"Can we get together soon?"

"I have to leave for Minnesota tomorrow and get settled in my apartment," he said. He seemed agitated. I was wondering what the problem could be when I blurted out I had to leave on Monday for Point.

"It doesn't seem fair…just when we," my voice trailed off.

Out of the blue came these words from Bill,

"I love you…I just want you to know I have always loved you," Bill said it softly and sincerely. He said it so plainly, it took me by surprise.

He continued, "I would not have felt right if I did not at least tell you… if I had not ever told you."

"I just want you to know that," he said quietly.

Sandra's car had crept out of the parking stall and was slowly pulling up to the steps of the Raveno. She pulled up right alongside of us.

I often wonder why I was so shy. My mind was racing with everything I felt and wanted to say.

"Say something, Barbara…anything," I thought to myself. Why I did not at least ask Bill for a ride home, I will never understand.

The thoughts were racing through my mind. "This should not be."

"We need to talk."

"I have to stay." "I have to go."

Wait a minute…stop the world. I want to get off and think about this for a long time…but there was no time that summer or ever again to tell Bill I felt the same.

Mercifully, the day came for me to transfer for my junior year at Stevens Point. My grandpa drove me to the college that was about seventy-five miles away and got me settled in off campus housing. I had three roommates in an officially approved campus building. I buckled down and after almost flunking out of college, my grades improved to 3.8. Once again, I was searching for just the "right" someone to be my forever love.

This was perhaps the "leaves turning down" in the esoteric, or perhaps transcendental painting Amigo Mary had done for me many years ago. My life was about to change in some profound ways.

10

Stevens Point University

I spent my junior year of college no farther than seventy-five miles from home. With my grades improving and being permanently away from home for the first time proved to be exciting. I started dating again. There were a few men I could have been serious about, but the timing and circumstances were set against a positive outcome.

My first semester was a growing up experience for me. I loved learning once again. Every class I took, I could not get enough of the in depth studies. Biology was my favorite. So was the instructor...who was a bachelor and handsome. I wrote lots of poetry about him. I actually gave the poems to him on the last day of class. I think he had many young college girls falling in love with him. He was kind and sent me a very nice thank you note!

I branched out and became much more independent this nineteenth year of my life. I ran for a class office. Though disappointed I was not elected, I loved the experience.

Viet Nam Sit-In Protest

There was a sit-in on campus that first semester. It was to protest the Viet Nam War. The Chancellor of the University wore a red vest so the students would recognize him and come to talk about the war. My roommates were going to the protest. I would not go.

I chose not to go because my sister's husband, my brother-in-law Joe, was in the army in Viet Nam. He was part of a reconnaissance team that would go on missions to see where the enemy was. He was in constant danger. So, how could I protest this war when I had a relative there? I could not. I would not. Not then....not ever. When our men are sent to war, the very least they should have to worry about is the love and support from home.

These soldiers had to endure the hatred and disrespect when they came back home after the war. They were scorned and shamed.

"How dare they do this," I thought. I still think that and I always will.

Second semester was starting and my grade point continued to climb. I had just changed my major to Elementary Education. I was taking classes that were inspiring me, challenging me and setting my vision for a career in teaching.

Impulsiveness Changes My Life

This is when I met the man I would marry. We dated and seemed to be propelled into a relationship neither one of us really wanted. I was on the rebound from dating a man I could easily have married. As I stated, the timing and circumstances just got in the way. Even though we both felt the same, it simply could not have been. Being on the rebound is never a good time to date anyone new.

I had never had sex or anything but kissing when I met the man who walked out of my life a short four years later. He asked if I could sneak out of my campus secured apartment. We could go to a motel, he suggested.

I jokingly told my roommates I was going to get married. I crawled out the window of our supervised campus apartment that night. We did go to a motel, but that encounter was laughable. He must not have been ready to stay in a motel room with a girl; I certainly was not ready! He ended up falling asleep watching TV. I could not sleep. Opening the nightstand drawer, I found the Bible. I began reading it until I could no longer stay awake. When I told my roommates the next day, they thought it was the funniest thing they ever heard.

I went to church the next day and marveled at the experience. I joined the Campus Crusade for Christ that week.

This man was determined we were to be married. After this second semester of my junior year, I dropped out of college. I moved back home to Menasha and began to work at the Banta Printing Company as I had done every summer for three years now.

He moved to Menasha and found an apartment downtown. We decided we should get married. That decision led to feelings it would be okay to experiment. What a hapless experience that was for me. The man I would be marrying knew nothing and I knew even less. He was too arrogant to care. We just never talked about how difficult it was or even how we should have waited. I should not have been surprised when he would one day walk out of my life, but I was.

My sweet mom knew something was not right because I was so pale and vomiting all the time. She had the same problem when pregnant with the four of her children. We were sitting at the breakfast table and I just came right out with it. She told me I did not have to marry him because I was pregnant. She said she already knew I was pregnant because I ate her whole jar of dill pickles in one sitting! Then of course, I vomited all the next day and for 8 ½ months after!

This Catholic man married me because that is what a good Catholic boy did when the girl he was dating was with child. Without thought, we got married. Even though my very liberal mom did not want this marriage to take place, she and my dad stood by me through it all.

After the wedding, we moved back to Point because my husband got a job there. We had a little campus apartment in the upstairs of a house. He worked. I vomited. Terrifyingly, for me, we would be leaving our University apartment. My husband's new job was in Beloit. Beloit was far away from everything I had grown to love...far away from family, friends and the University.

11

Becoming a Mother

My beautiful baby boy was born three weeks early. My water broke and off to the hospital we went. They gave me an epidural and more medication. I could not stay awake. The nurse tried to wake me up several times until the doctor came to scold me for sleeping. I wanted to stay awake but just could not.

Finally our son was born. We named him Steven John. My husband of less than a year; with his job transfer, found us three hours from my family. My mom wanted to be there for me, but was not able. We had Stevie baptized a month later. My family traveled all the way to Beloit for the baptism. I think my mom almost fainted when she saw how little food we had for guests arriving. They kindly bought us groceries before they left.

It was surreal that a few months before, I was happily heading to my senior year of college. I was beginning to gain confidence and looking forward to graduating. Now I was 200 miles from anything and every-thing I had ever known. I had a baby boy to care for with almost no money to get groceries. Then, I learned we were behind on rent and needed to find a cheaper apartment. We moved yet again. This was nearer to the store where my husband worked.

It was sad to leave that first little rental house as Stevie had turned one year old there. We had one of my husband's friends over for Stevie's first birthday. He was a very nice older bachelor. He spent Christmas with us, too. His name was Don. He was a very good friend.

Moving to a new Apartment

Now, this new apartment house was not a good house. It had rats in the basement and centipedes, too. I was down-in-the-dumps depressed. I tried to focus on Stevie and his needs. He was just turning two years old.

My sweet two year old was the first to inform me. He woke me up one morning saying,

"We have pets, Mommy!" "Can we keep them?"

I said, "Honey we don't have any pets."

"Come," he said, dragging me out of bed.

There under the dining room table was a family of mice eating the crumbs. I was terrified. The only thing I could bravely do was get rid of them. How? I could not bring myself to try to catch them. It was even more terrifying to let them have the run of the house. An idea came to me.

I grabbed the vacuum and sucked them all up. I took them outside in the vacuum bag and threw it all into the burn barrel in the back. I cried. Stevie cried, too.

We had a birthday party for Stevie when he turned two. We bought him a shiny red wagon. Another little boy down the street decided he wanted that wagon and just took it. I told him he could not have the wagon and lifted Stevie out.

Off went the wagon down the street. I ran to catch up with the little thief. I asked where he lived and he pointed one house away. I took him to the front door and rang the bell. A very large woman opened the door asking, "What are you doing with my grandson?" I told her the story.

She yelled, "Toad, get in the house!" Yes, his nickname was Toad. True story.

Out of the Mouths of Babes

My husband came home one evening with a couple in tow. The best I could offer them was a soda. Stevie just stared at the couple as he studied his hands and then their hands. He finally climbed up in his new friend's lap and wondered how she got the owie.

She had a thin white line across her bronze cheek. Stevie reached up and touched the scar on her cheek.

"Why is this white and you are brown," he asked touching the scar.

She very gently told him, "This is how black people heal when they have an owie."

With his curly blond hair and huge blue eyes looking right into her dark eyes he innocently said,

"When I grow up, I want to be black just like you."

We made fast friends with this lovely couple. They seemed so happy and affirming of each other. It was not the first time I began to compare my life with those around me. Everyone around me seemed so happy and successful. I had not been happy in my marriage for some time now.

My husband was coming home later each evening. Our love was not growing into a relationship I saw couples around us sharing. We barely talked with each other. Keeping control of my emotions was getting more difficult. I was miserable. I felt myself losing control of all my life's goals and dreams.

The Kidnapping

I decided I needed to finish my college education. An agreement with Point University made it possible to do my student teaching right in South Beloit. I interviewed and hired a woman to watch Stevie while I did my student teaching. Even though I had to walk a mile to school, I loved being with the children.

My biggest worry was to leave Stevie with someone I really did not know well. I came home that first day after teaching to find Stevie….. gone.

First, it was 4:00, then 5:00. I called the store to tell my husband. I thanked the Lord he could come right home. Now it was 6:00 and still no Stevie. I called the sitter's number several times with no answer. My heart was racing with panic. I asked my husband if we should call the police. Finally, the sitter came in with Stevie. I just sat and cried.

After doing a little research, it was not the first time this woman had done this. She even served some jail time for not returning with a child, even taking that child out of the state.

"What next, Lord, what next," I sobbed as I prayed that night.

Student Teaching

Next, Stevie went to a pastor's wife. My husband had to drive a mile in the opposite direction of the school to take him there in the morning. To tell the truth, I do not know how I made it through those four months of student teaching. It was one horrible story after the other.

First, the pastor's wife had a young daughter who was not happy to have Stevie there. Neither was the pastor's wife. They were getting in the car to get groceries and as the car was backing up, the daughter pushed Stevie out of the car. Stevie had a bandage on his nose when we picked him up. I cried and Stevie cried, too. He just clung to me as if he never wanted to let go.

Next, I had to find yet another sitter. The assistant manager's wife at the store where my husband worked said she would take Stevie. This was such a blessing at the time. She was so wonderful with children. Her name was Barbara, too! Stevie would be safe.

For the second part of my student teaching, I had a supervising teacher who did not mentor me as my first supervising teacher had. I came down with the Hong Kong flu. That is what they called it back then. This would have been in 1970. I had a high fever of 104. When I tried to walk, I was very weak and fell. There would be no way I could go to school as sick as I was.

I asked my husband to take my lesson plans with the teacher's manuals to school that morning. Apparently, the lesson plans had slipped inside the cover of the manual. When I returned to school after two days, the teacher asked why I did not send plans with the manuals.

"Well, I did," I explained it all to her. She said she never got them. I went to get the manuals, opened the cover, and there were the lesson plans. She simply did not care.

She decided I should not pass my student teaching. After achieving top grades in the first half of my student teaching, I felt a sense of defeat wondering if anything would ever work out. In a panic, I called my advisor at the college.

Well, my advisor came to the school all the way from Stevens Point to South Beloit. He spent much time talking with the teacher. He talked with the principal. He even talked to the teacher I had for the first part of my teaching experience. Everyone decided I should successfully pass student teaching. I was most grateful for this turn of events. It would have a great effect on my future career.

12

Too Many Moves

After the fourth move, two alone in Beloit, to South Beloit, I was weary of moving. It was traumatizing for me and upsetting for Stevie. We were on the move again. This time for a promotion for my husband. He was coming home late at night. I asked where he was. His excuses for working late were to get ahead in his career. I felt alone and afraid most of the time.

My husband finally got his promotion and we were moving once again. This was to a town sixteen miles away from South Beloit. There were three memories from that time. Stevie was almost three now, and we had to walk everywhere. I did not have a stroller for him and his wagon would not fit in the car, so we left it behind with Toad.

We needed food in the house. Stevie and I walked six blocks to a grocery store. I carefully counted out the seven dollars I had. In 1970, seven dollars bought one pound of hamburger, one gallon of milk, one box of cereal, one loaf of bread, a pound of margarine, and a can of corn and green beans. Maybe the stress was just too much. I must not have been thinking clearly. There were two bags of groceries to carry with a two year old in tow. After a few blocks, we both sat on the sidewalk and cried.

Not feeling well for some time now, I found a doctor within walking distance. Our neighbor in the other side of our duplex watched Stevie while I walked the mile with severe abdominal pain. The doctor ordered X-rays. They showed I had an abnormality of a third not fully developed kidney causing kidney stones.

Barely making it home, the doctor called. I had an allergic reaction to the iodine they injected into my blood stream to examine the kidney. This came back many years later to cause quite a scare.

The third and precious memory is that as Stevie turned three, we happened to turn the TV on one morning. We together watched the very first episode of Sesame Street! I was thrilled with the show as it encouraged children's love of learning. Stevie loved Big Bird!

My husband was still not coming home at night. I was depressed and not sure what to do. I called my mom to talk; but that was in the days of long distance calling charges. I had stopped calling home because of the expense. I decided it was time for me to finish my college education.

My dad intervened and reminded my husband that he made a promise. He had promised my dad on our wedding day that he would make sure I graduated from college. My dad paid for the last eighteen credits. I would not have graduated without his help.

Back to Stevens Point Once Again

My husband suggested I go back to Point to finish my education. He mentioned I could stay with his parents to save money. Leaving this town was not so hard because I would be going back to finish college.

We moved to my in-law's house. My sister-in-law watched Stevie until the semester was over. It was then that we called Stevie, Steven. It is what his paternal grandma called him. I did not drive, so I had to ride my husband's old bike to campus each day…come rain or shine!

My husband came to visit one weekend and disappeared into the basement with his mother. She was the first to know that my husband did not love me and wanted a divorce. She did not want to get into the middle of it and asked me to leave.

So, Steven and I moved once again. I had to finish a semester and a summer session to graduate. I settled into an apartment I shared with a young divorcee and her three year old. We took the boys to a day care in an upstairs apartment. I had no money, was late with the rent every month as I waited for my husband to send money. We had to leave because I could not keep up my end of the bargain to share the expenses.

We moved into a run down and spider filled apartment. I had to walk everywhere. I had no idea who I would get to watch Steven while I went to class.

My college roommate of just three years ago volunteered to take Steven. She was an answer to prayer as I had very little money. My dad was helping with the tuition. He thought my husband was sending rent and grocery money. He was not.

Ruth said she would love to have a little one to play with her son. This allowed me to finish the last of the nine credits I needed to graduate that summer of 1970.

Graduation Day

It was August now and my dad came to see me get my degree. He was so proud of me. I was the first of our family to have ever graduated college. All I could think was…for what purpose? The sacrifices of doing so brought me to my knees.

There were more moves that summer. I wanted to be with my husband, but that was not to be. I had no idea until my mother-in-law said she did not think her son loved me. Now uncertain of our future there was yet another move.

We moved into a trailer with a friend of my husband's. They were a young couple just married and willing to take us. We slept on a pull out couch. This would not work. This newlywed couple deserved privacy. One more time we went back to my childhood home.

Back Home to Doty Island

By the time Stevie turned three, we had lived in ten different places. Now, as we left Point, we moved in with my mom and dad for a while, then with my grandma. My mother decided after several months that I should be living with my husband and have him be responsible for us.

With each move Stevie and I made, I felt more defeated. Stevie was going through emotional turmoil from missing his daddy. Making it through each day became a burden. It seemed as if the burdens were piling up on my back like a ton of bricks.

It was not a very long stay in my childhood home on the Island. I would make one more attempt at saving my marriage; but where ever in the world was Eau Claire? My poor son. We were off once again to parts unknown…and my life was about to change again.

Eau Claire

My mom, with hope in her heart, had my brother drive me across the state to Eau Claire. I called my husband at his store. Yes, he finally got the position he had wanted at a brand new Woolworth store in a band new mall. Full of hope for a new start, I told him I had found an apartment and he could come home. We could work out whatever problems we had.

My hope was quickly shattered when he told me he had found another woman. They were living together. He would not be coming back.

It was a cold but sunny day in November. I found myself in a strange city and newly alone. Well not quite alone. I had Stevie! We were alone together in a strange city. We had just moved to Eau Claire and it might as well have been the other side of the world for us. In fact, it was just on the other side of the state.

I was 24 years old in early 1970. I had never seen an ocean and had never been out of the state but for the time camping with my grandparents when I was sixteen. That was the first time I had been any farther than 200 miles from home.

It was hard to process what was happening. My family was Roman Catholic and for me, marriage was for life. I had no idea what to do. What I did know was there was a Catholic church not far from us. I went to talk to the parish priest.

I told him I did not want to leave the Church. My husband left us. His advice was to find him and tell him he was a Catholic and needed to come back home to be with us.

That is what I did. I did not know where he was living with his girl-friend. His friend John from work knew where he was living. I rode with John to the apartment he was sharing with her. Then I just lost courage to climb those stairs and tell him what the priest had said.

John went up to tell my husband. He came back down looking terrified. He was so sorry to tell me that my husband was rolling on the floor laughing as he told him that was not going to happen! Back to the priest I went.

The new advice was that I should go talk to the priest at the Newman Center on the Eau Claire campus. He might be able to give me absolution. Taking my little boy's hand as we walked back to our apartment, I was thinking about what the priest told me. Why would it make a difference what priest I saw? Apparently, money was involved in all of it, but I did not know that for many more years to come.

A Precious Memory

The priest I had talked to encouraged me to come to church that Sunday. Stevie and I walked to the church for Mass. We were in a pew just behind a row of nuns. Stevie looked up at the altar and saw the crucifix with Jesus. He was studying it for quite some time. He did not yet know you should whisper in church.

With an outside voice he asked, "Why is Jesus wearing diapers?" I was a bit mortified as I looked up. There in the pew in front of us was a whole row of nuns laughing....silently laughing as their shoulders went up and down in unison!

Reality Sets In

Now, we would need some help to find food, friends and fellowship. We were truly all alone in a strange city. As we walked back to our apartment that morning, reality of our circumstances hit full force.

Anger and depression were threatening to undo clear thinking.

13

Lima Beans for Breakfast

So, "Now what," I thought. How did I ever get to here?

"Look," I began to shout to no one at all!

"Look at me," shouting louder now.

"You are looking at a Catholic school graduate, a college graduate, a mother…I do not belong here!" I was now whispering as angry, confused tears were spouting from my eyes.

I was in a strange city with no money, no job and alone with my son. It was a very dark time for me. I curled up in a ball on the couch with a cup of coffee. The next thing I remembered is my Stevie tugging on my leg telling me he was hungry. My coffee was ice cold and it was a day later. This jolted me out of my trance with panic.

Was my son okay? What did he do this whole time? I hurried into the kitchen to make him something to eat only to find the cupboard nearly empty…but for a can of beans. It was a can of Lima beans. Even the little milk we had was almost gone.

I heated the beans and told Stevie they were magic beans. If he ate the beans, he could make any wish he wanted and it would come true. All my precious little boy said was, "Okay, mommy."

Although the beans filled our stomachs that morning, to this very day, I have never eaten Lima beans again. I very much doubt Steve has either!

I walked to the duplex next to us to see where I could go for help. An elderly woman answered the door and invited us in. I told her my dilemma and she gave me $20 to buy groceries. I never felt more grateful for her kindness. The tears were flowing down my face as we left to buy the groceries.

Wait....we have to go back. Where was the grocery store? I had no idea how to get there. She kindly told us she did not drive and had no car. She said there was a city bus that stopped up at the corner. Stevie loved riding the bus. All I said to the bus driver was, please tell me when we are near to a grocery store.

That elderly woman was a retired schoolteacher. I called her Mrs. Fess. I shortened her name for Stevie. He loved his time doing puzzles and talking with Mrs. Fess. We now, not only knew someone, we had made a friend.

That is where I found myself alone with my four-year old son.

Knowing no one in Eau Claire but Mrs. Fess in the duplex next to me, I called my dad. He simply said, "Come home!"

I said, "No dad, I cannot do that." I just could not move again. I had a divorce pending and a four year old who needed me. My husband had given me some money so I could pay Mrs. Fess back. I had enough to pay rent and buy groceries.

To meet friends, I joined a Ladies' bowling league. Even though I had never bowled, that was the closet place for me to go in Eau Claire. I met a wonderful friend who helped me find a sitter for Stevie and a job at Penny's Department Store. I worked there through Christmas.

Christmas Comes and Goes

Stevie wanted to go home to see grandma and grandpa on Christmas Day. With the money I made at Penny's, I was able to call a cab to bring us to the bus depot. It had snowed during the night and the sidewalk was very slippery. Stevie was bundled into a heavy snowsuit as we approached the cab.

He slipped and his leg went under the cab. The cab driver had taken his foot off the pedal and the cab started to roll backward. It ran right over Stevie's leg. I was crying as I picked him up.

He said, "It doesn't hurt mommy!" We laugh about that to this day.

We took a bus to Appleton where my dad picked us up. Buses are the enemy for those who have motion sickness. I was sick the whole trip. Buses did not have bathrooms back then. The bus driver finally pulled over and found a container for me. As I recall, we had a wonderful Christmas.

My brother Bill drove us back to Eau Claire. I quit my job at J.C. Penny's as soon as the after Christmas sales were over and took a job at Snyder Drug Store. The boss hired me to manage the tobacco department. I never smoked anything in my life and here I was selling expensive cigars and pipe tobacco. During this time, I applied for my first teaching job. Oh, and I happened to meet the love of my life!

14

Our Wedding...A Lasting Love

Meeting Perry

After bowling one night, my friend Arlene and I walked through the bowling alley to the dance floor they had in those days. That is where I first saw my future second husband. Our eyes met, but there was no time for me or for him to say hello. On New Year's Eve, as fate would have it, we ended up meeting face to face at a college bar not far from my duplex.

We were married in Eau Claire in 1973. My dear friend, Arlene, was my maid of honor. She was the friend who had helped me when I needed a friend. She helped me find a sitter for Stevie when I did not know anyone in this sprawling college town.

When we began dating, I told Perry I was a Catholic. I told him all about the priest I had gone to see and that I wanted to remain Catholic.

He said, "Why not consider coming to Hope Lutheran?"

He had been attending that church since a boy.

"Maybe we could start out married life going to church and raising our future children in the Lutheran church," Perry ventured.

That is what we did. I took lessons to learn Lutheran Church beliefs. It was a requirement to join the church. Now I was Lutheran.

We had the sweetest little wedding. We invited my family who came from Menasha to attend, Perry's family, and our work friends. The reception was at the Ojibwa country golf course in a rural township. It was perfect in so many ways.

The only thing I can remember that did not go as well as I would have liked, was the amount of food Perry's five brothers could eat! No one seemed to mind and the food was delicious! We stayed in a local hotel in Eau Claire for the night. It was a simple wedding, quaint and special.

Learning to Drive

After years of walking and taking the bus, Perry thought it was time for me to learn to drive a car. After all, I inherited a car from my divorce. "Thank you very much," I told the Judge. He did not know I could not drive! We laugh over that to this day!

"You got the car and you don't even know how to drive," Perry joked. My 1967 Mustang had a stick shift. It was not in such great shape, but Perry was determined I would learn. There was the time he took me on the hills by the local college to practice. I had to continually shift the car or roll backwards down the hill! I begged him to take me home and just try again another day. He would not relent.

"You are either going to shift this car or you are going to roll back-ward and hit the car behind you," he calmly said.

It was madness and sadness at the same time! It must have been hilarious to watch. I eventually learned to maneuver the hills of Eau Claire. I passed my driving test the next week.

The first time driving alone, I had an accident. A very nice police officer wrote me a warning about keeping my eyes on the road. The truth is that after fifty years of driving, I am still not a very good driver.

A New Brother for Stevie

As Perry and I settled into a duplex in the township of Hallie, I was soon pregnant with our first and only child together. Our baby boy was born in 1974. He was almost 8 pounds and 21 inches. There are so many stories to tell about those years.

One memorable moment was when Stevie was in Kindergarten. He soon learned his last name was different from my new married name. He asked why his last name had to be different.

He surprised us one day when he asked if Perry would adopt him so he could have our last name. As it all turned out, that is what we did.

Stevie loved his brother Brent. Somedays they were the best of friends, and sometimes not. They managed to work things out over the years.

We were both working full time. Our lives were becoming increasingly hectic, but those first eight years were mostly happy adjusting years for us. The stories are endless as I am sure they are with so many families. Some may emerge here as I get on with my story.

There was a scare when baby Brent stopped eating and was vomiting often. The doctor who delivered him was Dr. Bates. He had me change his formula until we ran out of the different kinds that were available. Then came the tests for colitis, celiac disease and food allergies.

As each test came back negative, food allergies seemed the only possible cause. Dr. Bates put Brent on an experimental diet with all foods prohibited for a day. My poor baby could eat only one new food for twenty-four hours. We kept a chart to show what foods he could tolerate and which ones caused him vomiting and colic. Brent was always hungry and crying and I was a wreck! However, the technique worked and he was soon able to eat everything. He grew and thrived.

Finding the Teacher in Me

We had been renting when we thought we could do better owning our own home. Someone referred us to a local builder. He built our first home in 1974 for $21,500.

Our first house was awesome. We were so proud to be homeowners. Stevie seemed to enjoy school and his new friends. Brent was a bouncing baby boy. Settling into this neighborhood was a joy.

Soon I was applying for teaching positions. My first teaching job was a subbing position. Finishing out the year teaching sixth graders proved to be challenging, but was a stepping-stone to my next position.

Next, I was teaching fourth graders at Chestnut School. I learned many things that year. Children are the same the world over. I had great mentors on the staff. They helped me with ideas for classroom management and lesson planning.

The following year I took a Kindergarten position at the same school. Teaching Kindergarten is what I was born to do. I loved my kindergartners. I loved teaching the ABC's and 1 2 3's. I never wanted to leave the classroom ever!

Oh, and I finally forgave Sister Thelia, my 7th grade teaching nun from so many years ago. Her bulletin board prediction that I would become a Kindergarten teacher actually happened. Can you believe it?

Our Early Married Years

We were happily busy with raising the children, working and keeping up the house. We hired two or three moms who cared for children in their homes. Each time, there was a problem. We were running out of options when Perry suggested we take the boys to his mother's house. They were eight miles in the opposite direction, but we had no choice at the time. Perry's mom had after all, raised six boys!

It made our days a lot more peaceful...but much longer. It involved getting up at 5:00 am. Next, was getting the boys dressed and eating breakfast. Both of them rode the eight miles to grandma's house to drop Brent off with his diaper bag and toys. Then, a turn back to take Stevie to school.

I still had to get to school to teach. At 3:30, Perry picked Stevie up from school and then went to get Brent at his mom's house. I got home about the time he was getting back. We started supper, then baths, story time and off to bed. Only then did Perry and I have time for each other.

We were on the go all the time. One day our principal called me out of my classroom. She said she got a call from Halmstad School. My son had gotten hurt and would need to go to the hospital. Our principal, Gertie, took my class for the rest of the day.

I raced to Stevie's school and found him looking pale and sick in the nurse's room. He started vomiting, so I decided to take him right to the hospital. It was a good thing. He had fallen off the monkey bars on the playground. The doctor decided he had suffered a concussion.

He stayed in the hospital overnight and then at grandma's house for a couple days until he was feeling better.

Even though our days were long and exhausting, I had started a career I loved. We were experiencing what most families were. During the 1970's, inflation was high. We agreed it took both parents working to make ends meet.

Friends

During these days, we made several friends and always tried to have Friday night be our night out. I always felt guilty because I had such little time with the boys as it was.

Perry and I joined a couples bowling team. The couple was Deidra and Michael. We just had so much fun with them. Although they divorced after about five years, Deidra remained our friend.

Our years in Hallie were fulfilling years with work and neighborhood friends. We had eight mostly wonderful years. Instead of going out, we would walk to the neighborhood grocery store. It was a very little store. This is where we would buy a bottle of Annie Green Spring's Plum Hollow. It was a sweet...ah...affordable wine. Some my age might remember it. Plum Hollow was even cheaper than the popular Boone's Farm wine of the day. Perhaps the company that produced it passed into oblivion. I have not seen or heard about Annie Green Springs Plum Hollow since 1976. I would be first in line to buy it! Just for memory sake!

Perry had many friends in Eau Claire before we met. I was beginning to get to know his friends and what a joy they have been throughout our years. Dick and Carol had two young boys also. We supported each other through those rough days. Perry had gone to kindergarten with Dick and knew Carol since high school. Through Dick and Carol, we met more friends. We had a busy calendar filled with many good times.

Another Fire

We had a bad scare at our brand new house. The boys had a sleep over at grandma's house. We were having a housewarming party so our friends could see our new house.

We played games in the basement and gave out prizes. It was so much fun. I decorated the kitchen with candles on the table. Then, I set out snacks and sandwiches.

When we were in the basement playing the games, one of the candles burned down too far and started the tablecloth on fire. What a miracle I went to check on the food!

The fire was just about to ignite the drapes behind the table. Perry heard me scream his name and came flying up the stairs to help me put out the flames. By then everyone was in the kitchen. What could we do but make the best of it!

"Let's eat," I smiled. It put a rapid end to a flaming good party. We avoided what could have been a tragedy. In spite of the near catastrophe, everyone had a great time!

Neighborhood Friends for the Boys

Our boys were growing up fast. Steve was making friends. Most of the neighborhood boys played hockey. Steve played hockey too. He loved it. His best friend's name was Jeff, and his dad was the hockey coach.

I wrote a story about the years Steve played hockey. The name of the short story was *Horton Plays Hockey*. Brent would be ready for Kindergarten this year also.

Perry was at a dead end in his job and was certain this company would not be around much longer. I missed my family in Menasha. Our boys loved their friends and playing hockey.

Their friends and sports kept them happily busy. They played baseball outside in the summer months and hockey in the winter.

Although teaching was a joy as I grew in experience and confidence, I often shared with Perry how lonesome I was for my family. He was dissatisfied with his job and eager to find a new career. We began planning to move back to Menasha. Perry's family was not happy with that decision, but we were determined to move.

15

Back Home Again

The days of missing my family were soon to be over. I was longing to be close to my sister Cheryl. I missed my parents and brothers, too. We were making the trip to Menasha more frequently. It was a long trip for the boys and for two exhausted working parents! We would go home at my insistence every holiday. We could not miss Christmas, Easter, birthdays, and anniversaries. Perry grew weary and crabby about all the travel.

It was especially difficult in the winter when the roads were so icy. We would include stops to let Steve visit a couple days with his grandparents. They loved spending time with their grandson. They did not get to see his growing up years much. What eventually made all the travel worth it was establishing a closer relationship with my family.

Our house on Clement Avenue sold quickly. We were grateful for that because the decision to move was not an easy one. Perry had found a great job in Neenah and was traveling back to Hallie on the weekends. We were anxious for the move. As school would be ending for summer break in a week, it gave us time to adjust to a new house and neighborhood. It was important the boys get off to a good start in their new school. It ended up being emotionally harder for us than we thought it would be.

Finally, the day came to move to Menasha. At this busy and emotional time, I seemed oblivious to how this move was affecting the boys. They began quarrelling with each other. They would misbehave for no reason. With Perry gone during the week, I was doing all the packing, meeting with the real estate people and all the chasing with the boys. By the last day of that school year, things were totally out of control.

The same day the house sale was final in Hallie; it was moving day to the new house we had bought in Menasha. Perry and a friend moved some furniture in his truck. I packed the car full of everything from clothing to kitchen and bathroom stuff. The boys were crowded in the car as we pulled into grandma and grandpa's driveway. We were all crabby. Grandpa Claude was angry with me for taking his son and grandsons away "to the other side of the world." The good byes did not go well.

Once we were on the road, I scolded the boys for arguing.

"Aren't you excited to be going to a brand new house," I asked them.

That was the first realization that the boys did not think it was so much fun to move to Menasha. They were resentful of leaving their friends and family in Hallie. Their anger turned to tears.

Making a New Life

This is where our old life met our new life. We moved back to Menasha in 1979. We had made such a big move for the boys. We uprooted them from the only home and neighborhood they had grown to love. Hallie held so many memories for our sons. Steve was eleven years old now and Brent was five. Steve felt he had no friends in our neighborhood. Being an outgoing boy, finding friends seemed very hard for him.

Our street had many kids who were going to the same school the boys were. There was one boy Steve's age, but he did not want to make friends with Steve. Steve was having a hard time fitting in and we could not figure out why or what was going on with him. He was entering his pre-teen years and changing before our eyes. So was Brent.

Part of making a new life in Menasha was learning how everything had changed. I was forging new relationships with my parents, my sister and my brothers. One memory stands out above all others during this time.

A Journey of a Thousand Miles Begins with one Step

My sister Cheryl was about to have her third child. Our mom was going to stay with their kids when she went to the hospital. The time came for Cheryl to deliver. There was one problem, mom had been drinking for days and could not care for them.

Dad called me to come over to remove mom's contacts. I wore contact lenses at the time so knew how to remove them without hurting her eyes. I gently began asking her, "Mom, when is enough going to be enough?"

"Did you know you are a grandma again," I continued. "Cheryl had a baby boy tonight…your new grandson!"

With that, mom sat straight up in bed. "I have to be there with the kids," she said in a panicked voice. Then with more conviction she said, "If I drink again, I will die." I assured her the kids were with their other grandma so not to worry. She sobbed softly for a short while. I hugged her and left. My mom was ready to take that first step. She was about to renounce the grip alcoholism had on her life for almost thirty years....or die trying!

Mom never had another drink after that night, October 24, 1979. I remembered the prayers of my youth. The Hand of God had gently stroked our lives.

The Teacher Finds a New School

We went over to the neighborhood school to register the boys for the 1979-80 school year. The secretary of the school was a girl I grew up with on Oak Street so many years ago. It seemed like a lifetime ago. I told her I taught Kindergarten in Hallie before moving back to Menasha. The Principal of the school overheard me telling Hattie about this. He came out of his office and asked if I was interested in teaching Kindergarten.

Well, I really was not because I was determined to spend some time getting the boys adjusted to school and comfortable in their new house and city. The Principal continued to tell me a Kindergarten position was opening up after the school year started because the Kindergarten teacher was moving to Chicago.

He asked if I would at least sub for a few days for him to observe my teaching. Well, of course I would. I did. History was in the making! I accepted the Kindergarten job. I would be teaching Kindergarten in a few weeks....**in my own hometown!**

Personally, I loved my teaching job. I threw myself totally into my career. I developed my own Kindergarten curriculum during those years. My philosophy was five-year olds were eager to learn and needed exciting and challenging experiences. Children could learn anything! There was seldom a year I did not have at least 30 children in each morning and afternoon class. Yes, sixty children!

There was one year I had seventy-one children! It was challenging, but they learned everything they needed to learn. There is a saying that a child learns everything they need to learn in Kindergarten. I took that seriously. By the time they entered first grade, they all knew the ABC's and 123's! They had the beginning skills to be successful in every other subject. Many were already decoding sounds to make words and well into learning to read.

I developed Kindergarten learning centers. There was the Reading Center, Math Center, Social Studies Center, Science Center and the Free Play Center. On Monday, I would take the children to each Center and explain what they were to do for the week in each Center. I cut, pasted and laminated all of my own materials. Center time was a full forty minutes. That was a long time for a kindergartner to concentrate. However, each Center had hands-on learning activities. They cut, pasted, recited and had follow up activities for each assignment in the Center if they finished early.

The rest of the morning session I taught content, read to them, taught them how to interact politely and treat others with kindness. They had music, art and PE from special teachers.

My kindergartners would put on a play for our annual Mother's Day Program. They made all the invitations and decorations themselves. They did a short play where every one of my thirty kids in each session had a part. I admit I had to sometimes get creative and make up parts for them. They memorized their lines and some could read their lines.

There is a cute story many years later. One of my kindergartners, who was now an adult and a school Guidance Counselor, emailed me one day. She asked if I remembered the plays we put on in Kindergarten. "Mostly, yes," I said.

"Well, I remember you ran out of parts so when you got to me, I was a dog," she laughed. I guess not all of them appreciated their experience! That particular play had a family with kids, but I ran out of parts for each child. This play family inherited a dog, cat and some neighbors too, I think! This student was such a smart and capable child, I am sure she would have preferred a better part. I never wanted to show favorites. When choosing a play for the children, I would put all the kid's names in two separate bags....one for boys and one for girls! I would pull out a name and that is who got the part!

I taught every grade from Kindergarten to Sixth at some time during my career. I used the same philosophy for learning in these grades as I did my many years teaching Kindergarten.

This philosophy came in handy as I decided to coordinate the Summer School Program for our district. Summer School was once for those who needed extra help in a subject or was failing a grade. It was my dream to expand Summer School Programs to include Music, Art, Dance, Science, Geography, Acting and much more. Enrichment in these areas enhances a child's ability to learn in many ways. They learned to love to learn. As the Summer School Coordinator, I developed these experiential classes for students of all ages.

I did the hiring of the teachers, supervision, coordinating with the schools for rooms in which to teach. We had to expand to the high school because there were so many classes for the kids to take.

The experience of directing the Summer School Program stirred my interest in administration. I finished my degree for Elementary Administration and applied for several positons late into the summer. My district hired me as the Middle School Assistant Principal. Now, this was not only my most challenging experience ever, it required long hours. I was responsible for attendance, discipline and after school sports programs.

I was totally out of my area of expertise, but I must say; those two years were the best years of my career. Pre-teens were a delight. Yes, different from the early childhood years of teaching, but fascinating and challenging. Helping them to see there are consequences for the decisions they make, guiding them to find better ways to solve problems was rewarding in a very different way.

After two years of growing and learning about Middle School students, an Elementary Principal position opened. I loved doing that as well, but over the next five years of administration, I dreamed of moving on. The elementary school I taught and administrated was going to be completely demolished. A new, very modern and much larger elementary school was already well into the development phase. I decided it was time to explore new ideas. I retired from my career in teaching and administration after twenty-seven years.

16

A Lifelong Family Friendship

Mentioned in an earlier chapter of my story, the lives and adventures of two families began as neighbors on Oak Street in 1957. At present time, we have been friends for sixty-four years. The years from 1957 to present time witnessed happiness and joyful friendship. There was also a time of discontent, searching and moving on. By returning to the earlier years, you may more clearly see how lifelong friendships, my own decisions and shortcomings, and even family completes the circle of life.

1957 – 2012

It is hard to know where to begin after sixty-four years of lifelong memories. Where else but to start from the beginning?

I met my best friend for life when I knocked on the door of the first new family to move onto Oak Street in a very long time. Oak Street, in the middle of the block in the middle of Doty Island, and just off from the middle of Nicolet Boulevard, was a never changing neighborhood. Unless there was a death or sold properties, the houses are still there today. Although, the families have changed over time.

Even the house right next to ours where Mr. Meyer lived his entire life was about to change. Mr. Meyer died and Mrs. Meyer died several years before him. His son, Richard, inherited the house. He was young and not ready to manage it yet and decided to rent it out. That is when my life was about to change forever. The year was 1957 and I was eleven years old.

Never shy, I knocked on the door and introduced myself. Sandra came to the door and we just started on that day to be friends and never stopped. I taught her how to collect the big brown chestnuts that fell from the tree in their front yard. I used to name them because every one of those nuts was different…some lighter, some darker, some bigger, some smaller. Sometimes, when you forced open the spiny, lime-green shell, there were even "twins" to be found. Lining them up and studying them carefully, they each got a name. I arranged them into families. One family was Big Guy, Mama Nut, and the twins, Spotty and Glossy. They must have been fraternal twins! I think Sandra never met anyone like me, who at eleven years old, liked to name chestnuts.

Sandra quickly taught me how to play canasta, pinochle, sheepshead, poker and many more card games than I can remember these many years later. Once this family learned my mom and dad liked to play cards, they became fast friends, too. My mom and Margie even started a card club in the late 1950's. For many years, our two families gathered around the table and played poker. They played for real money, too. As my dad likes to say, "And, we still remained friends!"

These next-door neighbors certainly knew of my mom's periodic drinking episodes. They were a church going family just as we were. When mom was drinking, they must have just prayed for her and turned their faces away. There was never any gossip that I knew about, and the families remained friends until all passed on to eternity but my dad. My dad is still living as I write this memoir. He is 97 this year of 2021.

I am getting many decades ahead of the memories of those first years. The neighbor friends went to the UCC. We were devout Catholics. There were times I would go to church with Sandra. However, in those early years, I do not remember Sandra coming to church with me. There seemed to be an unspoken rule not to talk about the differences in beliefs. Well until decades later anyway.

Sandra and I did everything together during those years of our friendship. We explored Doty Island in the most amazing ways. One day we decided to walk around Lake Winnebago. The Fox River channels that connected with Lake Winnebago formed Doty Island.

Off we went on adventure after adventure. This time it was to start the journey around Lake Winnebago. We decided to start at the end of the boulevard that separated Menasha and Neenah. We got to the lake and started our mission to walk around the entire lake. We skirted around fences, walked in the water if we could not get past a fence, and even trespassed on many a property.

Finally, we ended up at the hospital. The hospital was only about two miles from where we started. We must have taken the wrong and long way around the lake by walking the shoreline. It seemed we had gone at least ten miles. While climbing the fence to get back on track, we both ripped our shorts…in the back! We took turns walking in front of each other as we only had one jacket to cover the rip…you know where!

We soon discovered we should have started our journey by going north and east rather than south and west. We never did make it around that lake. As we grew up, we learned that Lake Winnebago is 22 miles wide and almost 50 miles long. HA! That was only one of our many adventures during those years.

Skinny Dipping

Sandra and I went our separate ways when they moved to the Neenah side of Doty Island. We still saw each other every summer and when our parents got together to play cards. I attended Menasha High School and she went to Neenah High School. Menasha and Neenah were twin cities. The twin cities were a part of our state known as the Fox Valley.

That first summer living in Neenah, Sandra called and invited me over for a boat ride. She had just gotten her boating license. Their new house was just a block from the city marina with easy access to Lake Winnebago.

We put our swimsuits on and grabbed a towel. After leaving the marina, we anchored the boat in the channel leading into the lake. Her sister Katy jumped in first and I followed with a cannonball leap.

As no one was around to see us, Katy suggested we skinny-dip. She was handing me the top to her bikini as I was handing her the bottom of my bikini to put in the boat. As we were doing the exchange, we missed grabbing the suits. They sunk out of sight. We were giggling until we realized only one of us would be suited and one with only a towel! Katy got the suit and I got the towel.

It was a good thing our parents were happily talking and playing cards. We plastered ourselves against the wall and quietly sneaked past them. We have relived that memory many times during the years ahead.

Sandra and her family were singers. They could harmonize and were very good. They had dreams of appearing on the Lawrence Welk Show in the 1950's. Sandra sang in the high school choir and the drama club. She made many new friends. I tried everything from sports to drama and the forensics club.

Parting Ways...Staying Connected

When Sandra graduated from Neenah High School, she went right into the work force. She worked at the same printing company my dad worked for forty years. My dream was to go to college. There was a big argument in our family over my going to college. My mother was so against it, but my dad overruled her and off to college I went. It was a much needed social time for me, and more than enough challenge to learn new and amazing ideas.

I should have taken college more seriously than I did. I worked my way through college by working at the same company as my dad and Sandra. I worked three months during the summer and lived at home while attending a two-year college in Menasha. I then transferred to Stevens Point State College where I met my first husband.

Sandra was the first to get married. She married three weeks before me. Sandra married a sailor! I was her maid of honor, and was already with child. I married a young man three weeks later. By then Sandra was my matron-of-honor. We laughed at that because it sounded so much older than we were.

So much had changed for me in a matter of months! Although we cannot control all the circumstances of life, the many mistakes I made during this time left me wishing I had been more assertive. Life was one big mystery and I had not taken control of my destiny.

The magical thing was my best friend and I were married only three weeks apart. That in itself was magical.

Sandra was now part of the Navy Wives' Club. She and Charlie moved to the east coast for a year and then to Italy for three years. Her marriage was one adventure after another in the early days because Charlie was gone for months of sea duty.

However, my first marriage was unraveling. Stevie and I were in Eau Claire. This far away city would be our new home for many years. After just arriving in Eau Claire, my husband said he was living with another woman and wanted a divorce.

All the while, our parents, Joan and Jerry, Margie and Harvey spent their time as campsite owners and trailer neighbors. They spent time in Texas also. Where one couple went, the other followed. They were enjoying their retirement years together!

The Navy kept Sandra and Charlie busy moving from port to port over the next decade. We never lost contact, but our life experiences were very different. She had adjusted to the life of a military wife and mom. Their two girls, Carla and Wanda, adjusted well to all the moves.

The years Sandra was away were difficult years for me. I missed her friendship. She even missed my wedding day with Perry in 1973 while stationed in Italy. She was sad that my first marriage had ended, but Charlie was looking forward to meeting Perry...a sailor just like him!

I was a young divorcee in the early 70's. Within three years, I met and married the love of my life. Personality wise, we were two peas in a pod, really. Experientially, we were vastly different.

Perry was a sailor stationed in Scotland for three years. He had just gotten out of service when I met him. He was from a family of six boys. His mother was a hardworking and a hard loving woman. Perry's mom grew up on a farm. She married a man, who in hindsight, returned from WW II with PTSD. He also grew up in an alcoholic home. Life was hard for her and it was hard for the boys.

In contrast, even though my mom was an alcoholic, there was always support. We learned to communicate and talk things out. We loved each other unconditionally. Those two facts marshalled us through those difficult times. Perry and I moved back to Menasha in 1979.

That is the year my mom stopped drinking forever. Her health had deteriorated and she knew she would die if she did not stop. She loved her grandchildren so much. They alone were the reason she stopped cold turkey that day and never had another alcoholic drink again. She was sober for twenty-seven years before she died in 2006.

These were carefree years for both families. Watching our children grow, never far apart from all of our close times. There was joy, sorrows and challenges of life along the way that kept both families connected for almost forty years. Margie and Harvey both passed away and then my mom. My dad is the only living survivor of his generation of those years.

17

The Cottage Years

Sandra and Charlie eventually moved back and settled in Appleton near where we grew up. This brings our friendships with these lifelong friends, Charlie and Sandra, to the late 1980's. By now, Sandra and I were friends for over thirty years! Charlie and Perry became fast friends, too.

It was during these years I turned away from living a Christian life. We bought our cottage in 1987 and traveled to the cottages almost every weekend for twenty years. I never stopped praying, talking with the Lord, and believing the commitment I had made. Still, I was not living a Christian life.

The men loved to gather there each fall and engage in what they called The Hunt. If you are from the Midwest, more than likely you are a hunter or a cottage owner. The hunting party grew to ten at one point. Our small cottage became quite the camp for the men in those years.

Sandra and Charlie bought a cottage several years later. It was only about fifty miles from our cottage. Then Charlie's sister, Leah and her husband, bought a cottage a year or so later. Following suit, one of Sandra's younger sisters, Katy, and her husband bought a cottage. These four cottages were within a fifty-mile circle apart.

Let the North Woods Parties Begin

Oh, the parties we had! Those were the years of the Hunting Camp for the men. Those years were for the women also! The men had their Hunting Camps, and the women had their Getaway Weekends. We went from cabin to cabin with this group of friends for twenty years! There are too many stories to tell them all. Although one would have made us rich if we had only had a movie camera. You might agree we could have won the prize on America's Funniest Videos!

Sandra and Charlie were at our cottage for the weekend. They had their youngest daughter Wanda along this time. Sandra and Wanda were both large women. We decided to have a fishing day for the women. We got out the 12-foot fishing boat and motor. The men were protesting this decision, as they had wanted to go fishing. They decided we should prepare the fishing venture without the men's usual help.

We went to the shed and got the fishing poles and nets. We needed food, so packed some snacks and sodas. Next, we each had to have a life vest on. The three of us got into the boat and with the oars pushed ourselves out a ways so I could start the motor. Wanda was in the front, Sandra in the middle and I started the motor in the back of the boat.

In my excitement and anticipation for our fishing trip, I revved up the motor. The little boat's bow came up out of the water. For a short time anyway. Then, the bow started going down, down, down. As water poured into the boat, it submarined down further and flipped entirely over. As the three of us stood up completely drenched from head to foot, there were the fishing poles, tackle boxes, nets, soda cans all bobbing in the water around us! Then, there was the motor propeller completely out of the water spinning around.

Well, there were the men standing on shore with their arms crossed. We were laughing hysterically until we saw they did not think it was so funny.

In that moment, I felt panic. "Was anyone hurt," I wondered. No.

"Oh, no….the boat or motor must be ruined," was my next panicked thought. Nope.

Sadly, the men found no humor in it at all. For the rest of the day we all sulked around. As the years went by, we shared the story repeatedly. It was indeed the funniest thing anyone could ever have seen happen. It is certain, we would have won America's Funniest Videos grand prize.

After seven years, Sandra and Charlie came along to the cottage for the "Burning of the Mortgage" party. Now the cottage was officially ours! The deed was ours for real.

Losing My Brand New Rod and Reel...Really!

Then there was the time Perry bought me a brand new rod and reel. Of course, Sandra and I were off for another adventure on the lake. Part of Little Lake included an inlet to a smaller lake. After years of beavers damming up Little Lake, someone opened the inlet to the smaller lake. Now we had the smaller part of Little Lake to explore.

That is where Sandra and I often went turtle hunting. We would take our fishing nets and try to catch turtles. I do not remember ever actually catching a turtle, but we tried. This time we headed right out to the middle of the little lake. We fished and fished.

We drifted in a bit too close to shore, and as I cast my rod, it grabbed onto the weeds around the shore. I pulled and twisted and jerked but could not free it. I gave one enormous jerk and the hook came loose…flying right at Sandra. She ducked to the right and sure enough over went the boat.

Now we are in big trouble. It was deep and the line had wound all around my legs. Our tackle boxes were upside down floating in the water. We grabbed our tackle boxes and looked all over for my rod and reel. I pushed the boat while treading the water. Sandra pulled on it until we got to shore. I pulled all the fishing line and hooks off my pants. We got the boat turned over and got the motor started. We put the half-empty tackle boxes in the boat but could not find my rod and reel anywhere. It must have sunk out in the lake.

Very sadly, we started back to the cabin. I begged Sandra not to tell the men we had capsized the boat once again. I told her I would tell Perry in a few weeks. I did not have the heart to tell Perry the boat capsized on little lake while trying to save my newly acquired present from him. Sandra was certain they would know something was up!

"The guys are going to know something happened," Sandra said with doubt.

We got back and cleaned out the boat. We put the half-empty tackle boxes in the shed. Perry came out of the cabin and asked, "Where is your rod and reel?"

"Well…..you are not going to believe this but…well…umm….well I lost it in little lake!"

"My line got caught on something….and well…..it just went flying out of my hand and sunk!"

"Really?" "Well, you know that fish locator I bought?" "Let's go and look for it...do you remember about where you were?"

All I could manage was a quiet, "Sort of!"

We were off to little lake faster than I thought possible. We stopped with Perry using the fish locator. We found nothing there, but we were drifting closer to shore. There in the weeds was my rod and reel...and a whole lot of tackle.

"So, how did it get here?" he asked.

Well, the whole story came out sooner than I expected! Perry did not trust Sandra and me with the boat again. He bought a bigger boat so he and Charlie could fish to their utter content.

Getaway Weekends at the Cottages

For many more years, we traded off cottages each summer for Getaway Weekend. The men made plans to do guy stuff at one of the other cottages while we went for some fun. Two memories of those years are worth telling.

When it was my turn to have Getaway Weekend at our cottage, I decided to have a theme for the weekend. Being an avid amateur chef and having many Japanese dishes and utensils to use, I chose a Japanese theme. I taught at the Japanese language school and had gone to Japan when I was principal of the school. To enhance my student's learning, I collected many Japanese dishes and articles.

One of Sandra's sisters, Judy, came to help me prepare. I told her she was my sous chef. We left on Friday night and started to prepare for the meal early Friday morning. Preparation took hours, as I wanted it to be as authentic as possible. We chopped and chopped garlic, onions, veggies, and chicken. The friends all arrived just as we were finishing the cooking.

Almost everything we made was fresh from scratch. We made egg rolls and crabmeat Rangoon for appetizers, followed by won ton soup. The entrée was lemon chicken with rice. For a refreshing dessert, we made sake-dipped, sugared-coated green grapes. We finished by sipping hot sake as we shared the sage advice from our fortune cookies!

The next big memory of that weekend was going to the Indian Casinos that had just opened up. We had so much fun plugging the machines with nickels and quarters. When someone won a big jackpot, a Casino worker came and opened up the machine. Out poured quarters into a large plastic bucket. Gambling became a big part of Getaway Weekends after that!

A Snake in the Shed

There was the time Judy came to the cottage with me. We plugged up the toilet. With septic tanks, that can happen when too much toilet paper is used. We did not have cell phones back then, but did have a tabletop phone. I called Perry to ask what I should do.

"There's a snake out in the shed," he said.

Well if there was a snake in the shed, I sure was not going out there!

After a few calls back and forth, Perry, a bit exasperated, explained that a snake was a device to ream out the toilet. Judy helped me find what Perry described as a round container with a coil inside. It was pitch black outside and had snowed besides!

We were stumped, clueless actually! As we tried to figure out how to get the coil out of the round container, we could not stop laughing.

Tears rolled down our cheeks. We made more hysterical calls home to Perry.

Perry was past exasperation and getting a bit worried that his cottage would never be the same. He imagined his cottage being flooded and in need of extensive repair! He, not so calmly told us where to look for the lever that would release the coil. Success at last! We managed to feed the coil into the toilet and twist and turn until the clog came loose.

You will have to take my word for exactly how hilarious it must have been to watch two women trying to use a snake to ream out a toilet.

The next summer, Perry ripped the whole bathroom apart during a work weekend at the cottage. They installed a new shower, toilet and sink. They even replaced the flooring.

There were many more Getaway Weekend adventures at the three other cottages. Sandra's sister Katy's cottage was deep in the woods. It was part of the National Forest. There were bears...big black bears that like to visit her cottage. She also had an outdoor hot tub. We would all get our suits on and walk into the snowbanks surrounding the hot tub. When we were all extremely hot from sitting in the tub, we would jump out and do snow angels in the snow. No bears showed up to spoil our fun that night.

Sandra's cottage was closest to home. We always had a card game going and many trips to the Indian Casinos. Sandra's lake frontage was down a steep hill. We would take the boat out and row around the little lake and then sit outside in front of a huge roaring fire to roast marshmallows.

Leah's cottage, which was closest to ours...just about thirty miles away found us playing board games and card games. We always brought lots of food, but it was tradition to go out to eat on Friday night when the women arrived. The supper clubs of northern Wisconsin had the best steak and fish fries anyone could want. The weekend usually ended with long walks up the hilly, wooded wonderland, and long talks on her deck.

These exchanges of staying at each other's cottages went on for quite a few years. Each cottage weekend had its own unique memories... memories to last a lifetime.

Do you ever wonder if your friends know how much you love them? Sandra, Katy, Judy, Ruth and Leah blessed my life with fun and laughter.

Sandra and her family, our lifelong friends, were then and now surely loved.

18

Looking Back

The year was late 1985. The season of my discontent had been brewing for several years now. I was restless, knowing something was missing from my life. There was a strong feeling of wasted years, forgotten commitments, too long-neglected family connections. Choosing to travel for our next Getaway Weekend somehow did not seem as exciting as our past adventures together.

One reason for this restless and melancholy time might have been a growing interest to get back to my roots...my family. It seems friends took much of my free time during those years. I lacked focus and the importance of nurturing my family.

Now over fifteen years ago, I began to remember the burning desire to move back to my hometown. It was for reasons of family. I wanted my sons to know their aunts and uncles and put down a solid foundation. I started to confide my feelings during long walks with my sister.

She was a good listener and seemed to understand what was wrong. Soon after we settled in Menasha, Cheryl had asked me to go to a Catholic study of the Holy Spirit. I remember trying to connect the

Holy Spirit to my Catholic teaching. There was, at that time for me, a confused dead end as I tried to place the Spirit into the Trinity.

The first night of the study was like a Midwest tornado warning. Panic....then the eerie silence followed by wind, rain and hail. Most times that was all there was to a Midwest tornado; but there were times of great disaster that could level businesses and houses for miles.

The experience this seminar had on me was like being in the midst of a force I can hardly describe. Over the next twenty years, I experienced all of what a Midwest tornado could be at its worse.

I gave my life to Jesus after the Life in the Spirit seminar. Cheryl and Joe rented a large horse trough for the baptism that followed. It was winter in the Midwest so that worked well! I brought my son, Brent with me that night. He chose baptism, too.

There was a large spiritual revival in our area during this time. Evangelist Lowell Lundstrom came to Appleton during this evangelical revival period. We were encouraged to go. I asked both my sons if they would like to go. Now to my utter surprise, both my boys went up for the altar call and received Jesus as their Savior.

My son Steve went on to conquer alcohol addiction, marry and start a family. Our precious grandchildren were born during this time. Unexpectedly four years later, his wife asked for a divorce. Although this was traumatic and hurtful for him, he did not return to drinking. He moved out of state for a job in Oregon. He could not seem to make sense of what had happened.

After a few years, I could see how much his children needed him and encouraged him to come home. He finally moved back and tried to pick up the pieces of broken promises.

The rest will be his story to tell one day.

Our son Brent moved through those years between 1989 through the mid 2009 just being true to his faith, working hard, and searching for the love of his life. He wanted to marry and have a family of his own. This did not happen for him right away. He did marry for the first time in 2020 at the start of the Pandemic.

The rest will be his most fantastic story to tell one day.

During the time we were reconnecting with our lifelong friends, I was experiencing a different and profound change. It was like living in a parallel universe! Searching for a deeper meaning to life was on one side and a living a lifetime of magical memories on the other side.

The circle of our lives was beginning to take a turn toward completion.

New Little People in Our Lives

It was truly a looking back time. Looking back, Perry and I reflected on all those years of friendship. As now, we would be moving on to a new period of our lives.

These were busy grandparent days for us. The birth of our grandchildren enriched our lives. Cherishing and sharing them as they grew from babyhood into adulthood were remarkable years. Let me introduce you to our joys!

19

Our Grandchildren

Tianah Starr

The heartbeat of my life was the day my granddaughter was born. Her name was to be Tianah Starr. She was the most beautiful baby and sweetest child a grandma could hope to hold in her arms and heart. She had just turned two, and was learning how to put sentences together to express herself. I was playing a game with her. I would show her a book or some object and then ask her to close her eyes. When she opened them I asked, "Well, where did that book go?"

She looked at me with huge excited eyes and a pointing finger. With the cutest words ever to warm a grandma's heart, she said,

"It a-hind you, Grandma, It a-hind you!"

Sure enough, that is where it was. That is one of my sweetest memories of her. She loved books and we spent many an hour reading. She was an early reader and simply loved life.

She loved visits to the cottage also. One early spring day, the air was quite chilly. She begged me to let her go swimming. She was about four years old and had a heavy winter jacket on as we went out onto the dock. I wanted to show her how cold the water was....still icy near the shoreline. The next thing I remember is she took a leaping jump off the dock into the frigid water! I was so surprised she did that and I think she was, too!

As I carried her into the cottage, I stripped the clothes off her and put her in a warm shower. She changed clothes and we built a big fire in the fireplace. She warmed up eventually!

Tianah was a responsible big sister. When in middle school, she watched her brother and younger sister. She knew how to make lunch for them. She played with them, too. She put them to bed and was like a little mother taking care of them. My love for this girl knows no bounds.

Pierce Mitchell

Our next grandchild was Pierce Mitchell. He was perfect in every way. I loved how he loved to cuddle. He was a very quiet boy. I once told Perry....I have to play twenty questions with him before he will answer. I loved reading to him and teaching him the alphabet, numbers, shapes, and colors. He was a self-assured and responsible boy. He often took care of his younger sister when his mom was working. He loved being the big man of the family.

Pierce inherited my motion sickness. We were coming home from the cottage with him in the child protective seat when I turned to talk with him. He was pale and looking scared. I asked if he felt sick. He nodded his little head. Perry just barely got the car stopped and with me holding him outside the door, he vomited volumes. I explained motion sickness to him and that he would be okay. Calling it "getting car sick" because of the motion seemed to help him understand. I told him I had it too. I think he understood, but it scared him.

Pierce went on to love technology, taking things apart and building them again. He built his own computer from a kit when he was only eleven or twelve. He liked being on the tech crew for his school plays. He made friends easily. He has the same friends today that he made in high school.

One thing special about Pierce is he does not like fruit. As much as I prompted him to eat fruit whenever he was here for supper, he just shook his head, NO!

As far as I know, he has never eaten fruit, not even my apple pies! I would make just the crust of the pie for him with cinnamon and sugar on top! I love him just the same! Grandma's are like that.

20

The Last Getaway Weekend

Getting back to my story is not going to be easy. Years after attending that seminar with my sister, the tornado that hit my heart and my soul was heading to be one of the worst storms of my life.

These were the years of cottage fun, Weekend Getaways, and watching my beautiful grandchildren grow into sweet and kind adults. Twenty-seven years of teaching, raising the boys, and many times not being there when they needed me the most, tormented my thoughts. Way too many times.

At the end of these twenty years, during late 2004, we traveled for what was to be a very sad Getaway Weekend. It would be the last weekend I attend with my friends of fifty years.

As we were playing cards, the TV was on. A TV evangelist began to preach. Robert Schuller was a Protestant minister and popular TV personality on the Hour of Power program. He was famous for building the Crystal Cathedral.

As he was preaching, everything I had come to learn about Jesus being the only way to salvation came full force in front of me. However, on this evening, I was hearing a false Gospel. It may have been the son of Robert Schuller preaching. His preaching was void of talking about sin and repentance. It was replete with a social message.

"If you can dream it, you can own it," was the message.

"You deserve to be prosperous and have your desires fulfilled," he continued. Then the pitch for donations came next.

"Send your checks to the address you will see on your screen."

A voice inside just flew out of my mouth without ever a thought! "Well, that is not true," I simply and quietly said. Perhaps I was speaking my thoughts aloud. All I know is those words came out of my very soul. I looked up from my cards to see four women staring at me.

"What do you mean, that is not true," they said. "Don't you believe that," they asked.

Perhaps I was just shocked or incredulous they did believe it.

I am not sure, but I managed, "No, I do not."

"That is not what the Bible says," I managed in a whisper.

Confused and not wanting to argue, I fell silent. I know they were talking but I cannot remember a thing they said. It was my first experience of confrontation with my friends.

That weekend ended in a long drive home. I was certain they must not have understood me. Determined, I sat down at my computer and typed them an explanation of why I did not believe that message was accurate.

The letter was met with silence...varying degrees of silence from all but Sandra. My friend Sandra of over fifty years finally sent a response. I have saved every correspondence from the weeks after our silent confrontation. At the conclusion of all the corresponding back and forth, Sandra decided the only reason we had been friends for fifty years is we never talked about faith or politics.

This was a thoughtful time for me. It hit me like a lightning bolt to know I could not discuss my faith with my best friend! How did we manage to be so close for so many years and not be able to share the love of Jesus with each other? My dear husband sympathized with me. He was a wonderful listener and supported me. That weekend experience remains a barrier to the close friendship we five shared for so many years.

Why? I do ask that of myself often. Why?

In all honesty, I was deeply hurt at the time. Reflecting on it, I was not so much hurt as surprised. You come to know much about your close friends. It is rare today to have friends so close for well over fifty years. Surprise is not always a negative feeling. At that time of my life, it certainly was a very empty and lonely feeling.

Once I would have asked,

"What would it have hurt for them to ask me to explain about my new found faith...or to care enough about me to question even if they disagreed with me," I asked the Lord.

"What would it have hurt for them to come to church with me and hear what I heard and see what I saw," my mind questioned. Did they even care?

There was nothing but silence from them. In the first years after this experience, they continued to invite me for the Getaway Weekends. I found myself making honest but relieved excuses not to go.

I am sure their hearts were broken over all of this, too. However, I believed that as long as I did not talk about Jesus, I would be welcomed back into the group! I was also a coward, not wanting to be confrontational.

Two of the group have never talked about that evening. Nor have they independently reached out to me personally. It was the belief of Judy that her beliefs are private…no discussions.

I think the other two friends thought as Sandra. Religion is a subject best left silent in a friendship. One sweet friend of our group did try to reach out about fifteen years later, and it meant everything to me that she cared.

Lastly, Sandra. She is uncompromising in her sureness. She knows Jesus. She thinks the Bible can be interpreted differently…have different meanings to each individual. Sandra feels love is all that matters. That is true. Of all the virtues, love is supreme.

Sandra expressed it this way, "I might think one way, they another." Sandra saw these varying interpretations as merely differences…. there was no wrong or right way.

That in itself could be a problem. Differences in interpretation should be a starting point to discover truth. Although everyone wants to be right, differences in thought should be about seeking truth. You cannot refute truth. For God is ALL TRUTH.

We often ask for proof over the silliest things, but God's Word is all truth. Your eternity is at stake. All humanity will spend eternity somewhere. Learning the truth of what you believe is everything!

The Bible is not for private interpretation. Discussing the Bible does not have to be divisive. These few verses are but a tiny part of what we need to know to trust the Bible as the inerrant Word of God. (2Peter 1: 19-21; 2Timothy 3: 16; 2Timothy 4: 2-3)

If it is love that matters, what greater love is there that you would lay down your life for a friend? The willingness to talk about the inerrant word of God seems a loving thing to do for your friends. We must be willing to do this.

When you have the luxury of fifteen years to reflect, it is amazing how the Lord humbles you, cares for you. He leads us to truth. He leads us to His Word!

What have I learned?

Believing is not a feeling. My feelings about our interaction had nothing to do with it. I was feeling sorry for myself, saying things to myself such as,

"How could they reject me and my beliefs?"

"Why not talk about something as eternally important as faith and salvation?"

"Were they really my friends, after all?"

Can you see where I was wrong? I have no control over who will accept what I say and who will not. Jesus is the only one who can change hearts and lives.

It is never about YOU OR ME…it is all about HIM.

The Word of God will be confrontational. With open hearts and willing souls, it becomes a journey to search truth together! Then the

Word will fill each of us with His awesome love. Only God can judge people's hearts. I accept His judgment now and for eternity.

The Lord has preserved the love that I feel for our lifelong friends. The wonderful, crazy-funny times are memories filled with a love I still feel for each of them today.

21

Full Circle

My life experiences might be reflective of millions of other young girls growing up in an alcoholic home. I was on the fortunate side of that experience with a supportive father that decided to stay with his family no matter what. He was part of the "greatest generation" where commitment, loyalty, conviction and faith meant something. That made all the difference between defeat and hope.

Life and happiness is never a sure given! We are all born with an innate personality and sense of right and wrong. Those choices we make, even the choices we have no control to change, affect the life we will lead.

My life had experiences spanning rock bottom depression to over-the-top joy. Never would I have thought growing up, that my son and I would be eating Lima beans for breakfast.

There was always a helping hand. Faith helped one girl climb from despair to joy.

If reading the life story of an ordinary girl growing up in post-war years to the turn of the century gives someone hope for a better day; then writing my memoirs would be more than cathartic. It would be over-the-top joy.

It took many years for me to realize I could choose joy over life's failures, disappointments and impulsive decisions. As my life has come full circle, it is with a thankful heart that Jesus never stopped calling me to repentance with a love only God could give. It is my strong belief that faith is worth clinging to through all of life's trials.

My story continues.

Seeking and Finding Jesus AGAIN

It seems apparent to me that I had a friend in Jesus my whole life. I talked directly to Jesus since I was five years old. There were times in my life that I was discouraged, stubborn and angry. There was a disconnection between what I was doing and what I should have been doing. Never did those times reflect my turning away from my faith in Jesus. However, those times led to unfruitful, unsuccessful and damaging consequences.

At some time, all of us ask ourselves why. Why am I still at this point in my Christian life? Being a Christian was a part of who I was. By the early 2000's I was asking myself, "What happened"?

Almost twenty years before, I had accepted Jesus as my Lord and Savior and confirmed my commitment with baptism. I desired to have a lasting relationship with him. Earlier in my memoir, I mentioned turning my newfound belief aside for my own selfishness. Oh, I had all the excuses down pat, but the truth was I had not been living a Christian life. Jesus was not the focus of my life. I relegated Him to Sundays and an occasional Bible study here and there.

By late 2005, I had been retired from education four years. My sister Cheryl encouraged me to try a new church. She explained it was Bible centered and was something she had been missing. I was reluctant to go, but felt the same.

On a cold wintery night, I met my sister at church. The teaching was from the book of Isaiah. The Bible seemed to come alive as I learned about the history of Isaiah's day. I learned about his steadfast devotion to the voice of God. I felt like going again, not wanting to miss a single detail. Something tugged at my heart. It was Jesus calling me back to Him.

The following Wednesday, I just felt compelled to go back to this Bible teaching church. I finished the dishes and told Perry I was going to church.

"Okay, have a good time," he called after me.

"See you about 8:30," I called back.

This time I sat in the back of the church by myself. Cheryl and Joe had left for a stay at their home in Florida. The pastor continued in Isaiah 53.

Pastor read Isaiah 53:3-5 for the teaching on this night. I was wondering who that was crying next to me. It was not someone next to me; I was crying! Thankful I was further back in church that night, I could not stop the silent sobs coming from the very bottom of my being. I have thanked the Lord for this Bible teaching church many times, but not as much as that night when I met Jesus one more time.

The times that I experienced divine intervention in my life became apparent to me. There would be no other explanation for what was soon to happen in my life. The Lord needed to show me what was missing from my walk with Him. Without a doubt, it was repentance... and obedience.

It was not long after joining this church when Perry wanted to go with me. Neither of us have looked back. Perry had some of the same experience as I did, only in his own way.

A brighter day comes when you did all you could do. There was nothing left open to discuss. When I lay it all at the feet of Jesus, trusting in Him alone, my soul is secure. My spirit is uplifted. Accepting trials... reaching for God's grace is what is left.

From early 2006, the Lord called me back to a lasting relationship with Him. I have not left His side since that night.

God was not finished teaching me how to love Him more.

Epilogue

My Testimony

There were times I felt my life story had been complete. These memories have endured for seventy-five years.

The readers of this next part of my life will have to decide for themselves just what life is all about. If it takes you a bit by surprise, know that it had that same effect on my life. The impact of what happened next is a mystery even to me.

The Accident

Perry had just bought me a shiny green bicycle so we could ride together during retirement. He had a masculine looking black bike that he took for a spin right away. He would be retiring from his work life sometime within this next year.

Wanting to surprise Perry with my riding expertise, I decided that I would take my new bike for a spin before he got home from work. Surprising, even to me at the time, was how hard it was to get myself on the bike. Perry lowered my bike seat as far as it could go so my feet could touch the ground. This made it easier for me to stop safely. I thought if I got a bike with a lower, easy to step into frame, it would be a perfect ride for me. It was not easy to step over the bar. Lifting my foot over the pedals and onto the bike was an effort! Once on the bike, it was not as easy to steer it as I thought.

I was about two blocks from our house and decided to go down a dead-end road. I was going a bit fast when I realized there was a tree in the middle of the turn-around. I felt a bit out of control when I noticed a pothole looming directly in line with the bike. The bike tire caught the edge of the pothole and threw me forward off the bike. I hit a cement curb with my right knee. Then, my head found the ground with a thump.

I sat up more than a bit stunned. I then tried to stand up. Not a good thing. There was no feeling in my right leg and when putting pressure to stand up, I could not do it. Oh, oh I thought....Perry is not going to believe this!

Perry! I had to call someone for help. We had bought our first cell phones just a week ago. When deciding to take a bike ride, I grabbed the phone and put it in my pocket. Perry had programmed his work number into my phone just a few days before. I called him at work.

"Perry, I fell off my bike," I shakily told him.

"You weren't supposed to ride without me....are you okay?"

"I don't think so, I think I broke my leg," I told him with a sound he had never heard come from me. It was more like a confused cry.

"Did you call 911," was his next question.

"Oh, okay, I will call right now," I said.

"Where are you," he asked. Only but, for the Grace of God, did I even remember where I was.

I called 911. I told the operator that I had fallen off my bike and could not stand up. Apparently, the operator sent a police car and an ambulance. The police car missed the street where I was laying. It was because it was a dead end street about a block long; but there I lay yelling for that police car to turn around.

"I'm here! I'm here...come back!"

The police officer found me first. All I remember of that is the mosquitoes. I kept trying to shoo the mosquitoes away from her as she gently talked with me.

The ambulance arrived next with Perry right behind it. The paramedic must have seen I was by now going into shock. I vaguely remember him giving me something and adjusting the gurney in the ambulance. I remember I tried to listen for the siren but I do not remember hearing it. St. Elizabeth hospital was waiting to receive me. I was in and out of coherence as the hospital waited for a trauma orthopedic surgeon to come in to evaluate my injury.

Perry kept asking him what he thought. The doctor kept looking at the X-rays and shaking his head.

"I have only seen an injury like this once before and have had no experience doing the surgery," he said.

"This is a trauma injury and it looks like she has the start of compartment syndrome," he continued.

Perry began a barrage of questions, "What do you suggest we do?"

"What is compartment syndrome?"

"So, who can do the surgery, then?"

So it went, but I was blissfully medicated, and do not remember much else. I do remember the look on their faces. Grim.

"I would suggest you go to University Hospital."

"We can make arrangements for an ambulance to keep her stable during the transport," he explained.

What followed was a stream of questions about how this would all work. They finally decided that I would go in the ambulance with a nurse to look after me and keep me comfortable. I do remember wondering how much it would cost to take an ambulance one hundred miles to the University Hospital. Perry gave all his information to the doctor so that he could be in contact with the doctors at University.

The next thing I remember is talking to a doctor who filled up an entire doorway with his size! He started to explain that I had compartment syndrome and he would be my surgeon responsible to bring the swelling down in my leg before they could begin to fix the break.

"My name is Dr. Baer," he said. Well, he certainly was as big as a bear, I thought.

I woke up with an external fixator on my leg to stabilize the break. There were two huge incisions, one on the right side of my leg and one on the left side. There were tubes leading to a container that collected all the fluid from my lower leg.

The next doctor to see me was Dr. Lang, Orthopedic Traumatology. He was one of the three finest and top rated orthopedic surgeons in the United States. He was located in the University Medical School Orthopedic and Rehabilitation Medicine Center. I would be there for the next two weeks. Perry came to see me several times during those weeks, driving the 200-mile round trip to University Hospital each time.

There are quite a few stories, some horrifying, some comical, that I could tell about my two weeks there, but only one stands out as a life changing experience. That second surgery I had was to repair the break. Dr. Lang explained to me that I had a high plateau tibial fracture that resembled puzzle pieces.

They gave me more medications than my small frame could handle. The anesthetist must have been quite alarmed because I would not wake up after the five-hour surgery. They tried everything; I just would not wake up. I am not sure how long I was out, but I became aware of a faint voice saying,

"Barbara, Barbara can your hear me, can you feel this?"

The voice sounded so far away. I thought I was answering her, but I was not. I did eventually wake up. When back in my hospital room, the nurse gave me even more medications for pain through an IV. Really, I was feeling no pain.

The Black Blobs

As I was lying in bed that night, I could see black blobs on the ceiling. I watched them as they oozed down. Right before the black ooze was about to touch me, I woke up screaming. The nurses came running to my room.

"Please do not give me anymore medication, please, I feel so sick," I pleaded.

The nurses had to talk to Dr. Lang. He sat on the bed next to me and told me he was so sorry I had to endure that.

"We just have to keep you comfortable for a few days so you can get out of bed and walk again," he explained.

"I will, I promise, but with no more medication, please," I begged.

"Okay, then," he said. "But, you must let us know if you have any pain," he said.

Finally, he agreed I would have only Tylenol....without codeine!

When I fell asleep that night, it was without medication. I woke up in the middle of the night and asked for some paper and a pen. The nurse wanted me to sleep, but I told her Dr. Lang said I did not have to take any more medication. She went to check my chart and came back with paper and a pen. I began to write verse that night. I did not stop writing for several more days.

After two more days of therapy, walking with crutches up and down the hallways, I was ready to try steps.

"If you can go up and down steps with your crutches, you can be released," the therapist said.

"Go home," I asked with terror clearly in my voice. I cannot do this I thought. I just cannot do this.

I call her the "closer nurse" to this day. She came in and sat in a chair next to the bed.

"How long do you think you are staying here," she asked. "You have been here two weeks!"

"Dr. Lang never said anything about going home," I stubbornly said.

"Well, you are not staying here, either," she sternly replied none too gently.

Perry picked me up two days later.

When Perry got me settled, I was not the only one worried about being home.

"How are we going to handle this," he asked.

The most important take away from this crazy time for us is that I was inspired to keep writing. From my wheelchair pushed up to the computer, I finished three devotional booklets. My dad took pictures for the covers, and I kept writing. I edited, copyrighted, and published them. ***Writing for the Kingdom: Poetry for Daily Reflection***, ***Writing for the Kingdom: Praise and Glory***, and ***Writing for the Kingdom: The Spirit of Truth*** are the result of those years. My dad, who was eighty-five at the time, did the photography for each booklet. I assembled and printed them myself as I was recovering.

I needed months of rehabilitation when I left the hospital. The Lord put it on my heart to praise and honor Him during all this time. Feeling sorry for myself and moping was not an option. It was hard to see that at first, but it empowered me in His way, not my way.

A Total Recovery: Body, Soul and Spirit

Working on relationships with our adult children and grandchildren is an ongoing desire. The faith that God will never let them go is strong in our belief. They will each have their own story to tell. God is faithful to guide them to the Holy Spirit who will transform their lives. All they have to do is ASK!

It would have been difficult to relive each heartache, each human failure I brought on myself, even turning away for far too long from the Lord I serve and love. In all of those times, He has been the Hand reaching out.

What I have learned is you cannot go back. There is no going back for a truly converted Christian. Although it is our human nature wanting do-overs, there is no going back. This is what I know.

Jesus has forgiven me. He has straightened the path so many times when I did not even realize He was there. Graciously, He was.

Every Christian experiences accepting Jesus personally. What had been missing for many years for me was repentance first at the foot of the cross. It is impossible to know Jesus without accepting His sacrifice for us. His love for each of us individually, exposes our grievous sins. Our sorrow leads us to Him. We find Him in his Word, the Bible. His Word became the daily necessity of our lives. Perry and I are both eternally grateful.

Never Looking Back

As always, there is so much of a lifetime to share. Some of it elusive... a bit like protecting our hearts from breaking. What I know from my life experiences is there will never be a circumstance, condition, or relationship on this earth that would cause me to longing look back for do-overs.

I care nothing for do-overs...those missed opportunities, agonizing mistakes, sinful choices, miraculous experiences, enjoyment, employment, contentment, or any tug-at-the-heart experience.

They were all a part of my life...only until I gave my life away. The old woman is dead within me. The new woman is looking toward Eternal Treasures. Look up! Jesus will be waiting at the finish line.

Note from the Author

I have found that writing my memoir has been joy and challenge both. If you found it interesting how growing up in a small town after WW II varied from the times you grew up, I am delighted!

My growing up years would not be the same as yours because my circumstances and my personality are unique to me. Your growing up years would reflect your unique personality. Your life experiences would highlight that uniqueness.

Being a teacher for many years, I would love to use my story with pre-teens and teenagers to help them learn to compare and contrast, research and draw conclusions. These are thinking skills needed throughout life for making decisions and discerning the best path to a successful life journey.

I make myself available to your school or organization to do a workshop with pre-teens and teenagers who want to explore writing, decision making and setting life-long goals.

I am the author of **Writing for the Kingdom: Praise and Glory** and **Lima Beans for Breakfast**.

I am available to the following groups for workshops:

- **Home-school parents**
- **Public and parochial schools**
- **Summer school coordinators**
- **Librarians**
- **Bookstores**
- **Boy's and Girl's Clubs**

You can contact me at the following email address.

qtile.bd@gmail.com

You can purchase and download *Lima Beans for Breakfast* from my website.

www.outskirtspress.com/limabeansforbreakfast

www.outskirtspress.com/writingforthekingdom

Note to the Reader

This is a true story. All experiences are true to life and as accurately described as possible. Some first names are pseudonyms to protect privacy.

The contents of this book are solely the work of the author.

Please contact the author with any inquiries, permissions or interest in workshops.

qtile.bd@gmail.com

Barbara Drinkwine, Author

CPSIA information can be obtained
at www.ICGtesting.com
Printed in the USA
BVHW081448291121
622773BV00003B/123